"For many, the imagination is sync something to outgrow as we matur church an incredible service in liftin the Christian life. Their insights help us realize that the nations are engaged that we are able to live out our calling faithfully in every arena of life."

    David H. Kim, Executive Director, Center for Faith and Work, Redeemer Presbyterian Church, New York City; author, *Glimpses of a Greater Glory* and *20 and Something*

"Imagination—a gift from God—is not just for daydream or fantasy. It's critical to objective recall and idea development. A thought-provoking gem, this is a must-read."

    Bob Doll, Chief Equity Strategist and Senior Portfolio Manager, Nuveen Asset Management

"Defenses of the imagination are somewhat common, but this one combines the perspectives of a literary scholar and a biblical expositor. The result is a unique defense of the imagination. The book is reader friendly, and the defense of the imagination is comprehensive. A particular strength is the demonstration of how the imagination relates to the Bible."

    Leland Ryken, Emeritus Professor of English, Wheaton College

"This is a biblically grounded, down-to-earth, and eminently accessible book. It deserves to be widely read."

    Jeremy S. Begbie, Thomas A. Langford Research Professor of Theology, Duke University; author, *Resounding Truth: Christian Wisdom in the World of Music* and *Music Modernity and God*

"Veith and Ristuccia offer practical steps for keeping our imaginations captive to Christ. Veith clearly defines imagination and explains its role in our daily lives, tracing our understanding of imagination through key figures in history. Ristuccia insightfully exposits sections of Ezekiel, showing how God engages our imagination to reveal his character and plan of salvation. Reading this book will help you, as it helped me, fulfill the great command to love God with all your mind. I highly recommend it."

    Danielle Sallade, Campus Minister, Princeton Evangelical Fellowship, Princeton University

"Veith and Ristuccia have teamed up to give us a mind-stretching introduction to imagination from a biblical perspective. As I read this book, I learned things I had never thought about before and was often made to stop, think, and pray."

    Ajith Fernando, Teaching Director, Youth for Christ, Sri Lanka

Imagination Redeemed

Imagination Redeemed

Glorifying God with a
Neglected Part of Your Mind

Gene Edward Veith Jr.
and Matthew P. Ristuccia

CROSSWAY
WHEATON, ILLINOIS

Imagination Redeemed: Glorifying God with a Neglected Part of Your Mind

Copyright © 2015 by Gene Edward Veith Jr. and Matthew P. Ristuccia

Published by Crossway
    1300 Crescent Street
    Wheaton, Illinois 60187

Cover design: Faceout Studio

First printing 2014

Printed in the United States of America

Unless otherwise indicated, Scripture quotations are from the ESV® Bible (*The Holy Bible, English Standard Version*®), copyright © 2001 by Crossway. 2011 Text Edition. Used by permission. All rights reserved.

Scripture quotations marked AT are the author's translation.

Scripture quotations marked KJV are from the *King James Version* of the Bible.

Scripture quotations marked NIV are taken from *The Holy Bible, New International Version*®, NIV®. Copyright © 1973, 1978, 1984, 2011 by Biblica, Inc.™ Used by permission. All rights reserved worldwide.

Scripture references marked NLT are from *The Holy Bible, New Living Translation*, copyright © 1996, 2004. Used by permission of Tyndale House Publishers, Inc., Wheaton, Ill., 60189. All rights reserved.

All emphases in Scripture quotations have been added by the authors.

Trade paperback ISBN: 978-1-4335-4183-4
ePub ISBN: 978-1-4335-4186-5
PDF ISBN: 978-1-4335-4184-1
Mobipocket ISBN: 978-1-4335-4185-8

Library of Congress Cataloging-in-Publication Data
Veith, Gene Edward, 1951-
   Imagination redeemed : glorifying God with a neglected part of your
mind / Gene Edward Veith and Matthew P. Ristuccia.
     pages cm
   Includes bibliographical references and index.
   ISBN 978-1-4335-4183-4 (tp)
   1. Imagination—Religious aspects—Christianity. 2. Thought and
thinking—Religious aspects—Christianity. I. Title.
BR115.I6V45   2014
233'.5—dc23   2014015322

Crossway is a publishing ministry of Good News Publishers.

VP		24	23	22	21	20	19	18	17	16	15	14
15	14	13	12	11	10	9	8	7	6	5	4	3	2	1

To
Jackie,
our daughters, son, sons-in-law,
and our grandchildren

and

To
Karen,
our sons and daughters-in-law,
and our grandchildren.

Without you life would be unimaginable

Contents

Introduction

This book had its genesis when Matthew Ristuccia, pastor of Stone Hill Church of Princeton (formerly Westerly Road Church), gave the Biblical Emphasis Week lectures at my school, Patrick Henry College. He spoke on the book of Ezekiel, showing how it addresses the issues of the imagination. I had never heard that take before. As a literature professor, I was interested, naturally enough, in the imagination, had studied its literary manifestations, and knew about the imaginative biblical meditations that shaped Christian poetry. Matt was providing, for me, the missing links to the Bible and the Christian life. In the course of our subsequent conversations, he referred to John Piper's book *Think*, about "the life of the mind and the love of God"; and to Matthew Eliott's *Feel*, about the proper role of emotions in the Christian's life. Matt saw a gap that begged to be filled, a book he initially entitled *Imagine*. After a while, we resolved to collaborate in writing that book. My part is to write about the imagination as a whole, drawing on what I know about the arts and literature, philosophy and psychology. His part is to show how all of this plays out in the Word of God, specifically in the visions of Ezekiel.

Most writing collaborations involve smoothing out differences of style and trying to make it impossible to tell who wrote which part. That entails dropping first-person references (what "I" did and what happened to "me"), getting rid of our individual voices (since the author is a collective entity), and creating the illusion of single authorship (which isn't even true, as the title page makes clear). We will experiment with a different approach throughout most of this book. I (Gene) will begin each chapter, exploring the topic from my vantage point, then I will turn it over to Matt. And then the two of us will take it up again with some practical conclusions.

Also, the chapters will be organized around the mental exercise that gave us a classic form of Bible meditation and a great deal of Christian literature: the engagement of the imagination, the understanding, and the will—though not in that order. I have written the so-called analysis, addressing the understanding. Matt has written the composition, addressing the imagination through interaction with the Word of God. Each chapter ends with a colloquy, addressing the will so as to motivate you to carry out these truths in your own life, and, as with all classic meditations, with prayer.

Imagination:
The Mind's Eye

The heavens were opened, and I saw visions of God.

Ezekiel 1:1

Fine nets and stratagems to catch us in,
Bibles laid open, millions of surprises.

"Sin" (I), George Herbert

From Gene

Imagination is simply the power of the mind to form a mental image, that is, to think in pictures or other sensory representations. The imagination is at work when you use your memory. (What did you have for dinner yesterday? Do you remember what it looked like? How it tasted? You are using your imagination.) You use your imagination when you plan to do something in the future. (What is on your to-do list for tomorrow? What are you going to have to take care of at work? Do you have errands to run? Notice the mental pictures that come to mind.) Imagination lets us relive the past and anticipate the future. And it takes up much of our present. We use our imaginations when we daydream and fantasize, to be sure, but also when we just think about things.

Reading requires the imagination, which is true whether you are reading a narrative ("It was a dark and stormy night"; "Abraham Lincoln was born in a log cabin in 1809"; "Two people were killed Saturday night when their car ran out of control and struck a tree") or an exposition of ideas ("Examples of the economic factors would include the housing market, the automobile industry, and Wall Street"; "Plato explains his philosophy with the analogy of people chained up inside a cave"; "Christ died for sinners"). Notice how much you have been using your imagination just reading this paragraph.

So imagination is this faculty we all have of conjuring up pictures in our minds. That's all it is. Many treatments of the topic glamorize and mystify the imagination. It is associated with the fine arts and artistic genius. The imagination, we are told, is a matter of creativity. The whole concept is often presented as if it were some special talent held only by a few or perhaps as if it might be cultivated if you work hard enough at it. We ordinary folks are exhorted to "be creative!" and to "use your imagination!" But, failing to measure up to the great poets and inventors, we might reasonably conclude, "I don't really have much imagination." But you do! If I say, "Think of a tree," and you can do that, you have imagination. It is true that artists work with their imaginations and address ours. And since we can imagine things that do not currently exist (think of a tree with blue leaves), it is the faculty behind creativity. These are applications of imagination, as we shall see, but the ability itself is a God-given power of the human mind that is so common, so ordinary, that we take it for granted.

When we think of the human mind, we usually think of the intellect (reason), emotions (feelings), and possibly the will (desires, choices). Those are other mental faculties that we have. I suspect, though, that our conscious minds are occupied far more with our imaginations than with these other faculties. In fact, the imagination often provides the subject matter and the impetus for our reasoning, our feelings, and our choices. Strangely, though, we have tended to overlook the imagination and the role it plays in our thinking and in our lives.

This is certainly true of Christians, who have done much with epistemology (the study of how we know) and have long debated the role and limits of reason and the will. Actually, Christians of the past had quite a bit to say about the imagination, as we shall see, but it is something of a forgotten category in contemporary Christianity.

Some might say that Christians, or Protestants, or evangelicals are "suspicious of the imagination." But, again, in the sense that we are using the word, the imagination is not something we can choose to employ. The issue is not whether imagination is good or bad, useful or not, or something we should or should not cultivate. We cannot help but use our imaginations. This is the way God made our minds to function. But it will help us greatly to reflect upon the role and limits and possibilities of the imagination, just as we have with reason and our other mental powers.

One reason Christians may have shied away from emphasizing the imagination is biblical texts like this: "And God saw that the wickedness of man was great in the earth, and that every *imagination* of the thoughts of his heart *was only evil continually*" (Gen. 6:5 KJV). In this text, the reference is to the human condition that provoked the flood, and so, one might argue, what connection is there? That was then, and this is now. But there are plenty of other biblical warnings about the imagination, including Jeremiah's caution about "walk[ing] in the imagination of [our] hearts" (Jer. 13:10, and six other places in that book), and Paul's assessment that sinful human beings have become "vain in their imaginations" (Rom. 1:21 KJV). To be sure, the imagination—like reason, emotions, and the will— is fallen. Our knowledge of God must come from his revelation of himself to us, that is, through his Word, which may in no way be replaced by human reason, emotion, will, or imagination. Imagination is indeed the source of all idolatry (the "graven images" that begin with mental images) and all false religions (which we imaginatively construct to evade the true God).

Furthermore, we must "walk" by the Word of God; that is, we must live according to God's revelation in Scripture rather than by our own reasonings, feelings, choices, or imaginings. Jesus himself warns us about murdering and committing adultery in our heart (Matt. 5: 21–30). Imaginary fantasies about illicit sex or about harming someone are sinful, even if they are never acted upon. This is because they disclose and aggravate a sinful heart.

But just because the imagination can be the source of idolatry and other sins is no reason to ignore it. That the imagination can be used for evil means that Christians dare not ignore it. We must discipline, disciple, and sanctify our imaginations. We are to "take every thought captive to obey Christ" (2 Cor. 10:5), and that must include the thoughts we imagine. This can be done, above all, by saturating our imaginations with the Word of God. The Bible directly addresses the imagination in its narratives, descriptions, and vivid language.

Notice how your imagination is working as you read these passages, taken nearly at random:

> In the beginning, God created the heavens and the earth. The earth was without form and void, and darkness was over the face of the deep. And the Spirit of God was hovering over the face of the waters. (Gen. 1:1–2)

> Blessed is the man
> who walks not in the counsel of the wicked,
> nor stands in the way of sinners,
> nor sits in the seat of scoffers;
> but his delight is in the law of the LORD,
> and on his law he meditates day and night.

> He is like a tree
> planted by streams of water

that yields its fruit in its season,
    and its leaf does not wither.
In all that he does, he prospers.
The wicked are not so,
    but are like chaff that the wind drives away. (Ps. 1:1–4)

That same day Jesus went out of the house and sat beside the sea. And great crowds gathered about him, so that he got into a boat and sat down. And the whole crowd stood on the beach. And he told them many things in parables, saying: "A sower went out to sow. And as he sowed, some seeds fell along the path, and the birds came and devoured them. Other seeds fell on rocky ground, where they did not have much soil, and immediately they sprang up, since they had no depth of soil, but when the sun rose they were scorched. And since they had no root, they withered away. Other seeds fell among thorns, and the thorns grew up and choked them. Other seeds fell on good soil and produced grain, some a hundredfold, some sixty, some thirty. He who has ears, let him hear." (Matt. 13:1–9)

If I speak in the tongues of men and of angels, but have not love, I am a noisy gong or a clanging cymbal. And if I have prophetic powers, and understand all mysteries and all knowledge, and if I have all faith, so as to remove mountains, but have not love, I am nothing. If I give away all I have, and if I deliver up my body to be burned, but have not love, I gain nothing. (1 Cor. 13:1–3)

Just reading those passages fills our minds with mental images of light and darkness, trees planted by streams of water, great crowds, a boat anchored by the shore, a sower in the fields, noisy gongs and clanging cymbals, what it would be like to give away everything including one's life at the stake, and the personal associations we each have with love. The Bible also gives directives for how we can use our imaginations in a holy way. For example, when the apostle

Paul enjoins us to "rejoice with those who rejoice" and to "weep with those who weep" (Rom. 12:15), he is calling for an act of imagination known as "empathy," imaginatively identifying with other human beings to the point of feeling their emotions.

In practice, the different faculties of our minds work together seamlessly, and the imagination plays an important role in integrating our ideas and our feelings, the outer world and our inmost selves. Imagination bridges the rational powers and the emotional center of our being.

Indeed, God reaches us by connecting to our imaginations. And appealing to the imagination is a way we can reach others. C. S. Lewis tells about how God worked not simply through his intellect but also through his imagination to bring him to faith. T. S. Eliot struggled with the fragmentation of the intellect and the emotions, which he found to be characteristic of the modern age. He found wholeness in the Christian imagination, in works of Christian literature that would eventually lead to his conversion. When God captures our imagination, he captures the rest of our mind, including our understanding and our will.

Developing a Christian imagination can play an important role in our spiritual growth. A godly imagination can help us meditate on the Word of God, pray with fervency, cultivate a corporate culture of grace, and grow through personal sanctification (recognizing sin's inventions, fighting temptation, putting off the old and putting on the new, loving our neighbors). When we read the Bible with our imaginations fully engaged, the biblical truths become personal. And a sanctified imagination can help us direct our choices and set plans toward a Christ-centered future.

To become conscious of the imagination and to reflect on its powers and uses is to be filled with gratitude for an astonishing gift of God, a reflection of the mind of God himself whose creativity went so far as to make us according to his image and his imagination.

Ezekiel and the Imagination

An Unexpected Encounter

My first experience with Ezekiel goes back to my pre-Christian days. At the request of my parents, who were distraught with my late-adolescent mutinies, I postponed entrance to university and spent a gap year in England attending a "public school," the British equivalent of an American prep school. It was there, in the tiny, two-desk study that I shared with a roommate from Iran, that I opened a Bible for the first time in my life.

I had heard of the Bible many times before, but I had never thought it was important enough to read. To be honest, I thought it was dangerous: "ancient literature, the kind of thing too many people have died over. Don't go there." But God used common grace to his advantage and mine. You see, I had a keen interest in English literature and recently had become intrigued with a curious seventeenth-century book called *The Pilgrim's Progress*. "Odd," I commented to myself when I saw the title, "what on earth does progress have to do with a pilgrim?" I wish I could say that I then immersed myself in the text, but, alas, I was much more captured by the yellow cover of the Penguin Books edition: a spiral maze, various people walking, the so-called Celestial City at the center. "Cool." Next to it on the library stack was a different edition, one that contained marginal glosses unlike anything I had ever seen, peculiar notations such as "Is. 64:6."

"What does "Is. 64:6 mean?" I later asked my roommate. He was studying for his A-level exam in English literature, so I figured he should know. And he did.

"Oh, 'Is. 64:6' is a reference to some passage in the Bible."

"Oh, okay." I pretended that I understood, although I didn't. But in that moment, the idea birthed full-term in my mind: "Matthew, if you're serious about English lit, you should really read the Bible."

I attempted to do so a few days later. Still having no idea what "Is. 64:6" meant, and all the while intrigued by what the Bible might contain, while I was alone in the study mixing up some instant coffee, I noticed *The Holy Bible* on the shelf above my roommate's desk. I decided I would take a look. I opened to the table of contents and found there a long list of unusual names. I recognized Genesis, to be sure, but names such as Numbers (what on earth is that about—ancient Hebrew arithmetic?) and Judges (key moments in jurisprudence?) sounded strange, almost cultish. They put me off.

But then I noticed something with which I was familiar: Ezekiel. "Oh," I said to myself, "that must be the same Ezekiel who 'saw da wheel.'" Years before, during my junior high years, I had sung in a community choir, and one of our favorite songs was the spiritual, "Ezekiel saw da wheel, way up in da middle of de air." It was lively, it had great parts, and the words had stuck with me.

So I turned to Ezekiel on page 643 and began to read. But phrases such as "son of Buzi" and "living creatures" and "the gleaming of beryl" and "wheel within a wheel" bewildered me. I had no idea what was going on, and the more I read, the more jumbled I became. "Well, that's it for the Bible," I commented. "I've given it a try, and it makes no sense. It's not worth the bother."

Such providential irony! Today Ezekiel is among my favorite books in the divine canon. And I am just one in a long line of people who have studied and preached and loved what this eccentric prophet has bequeathed to us. Take John Calvin; he was in the midst of preaching an in-depth series (did Calvin ever preach a lite series?) on Ezekiel when he died. A few centuries later, the great American Puritan Cotton Mather turned to Ezekiel 24 in order to shape his thoughts for what would be one of his most moving sermons, "The Loss of a Desirable Relative, Lamented and Improved," given at the funeral of his beloved wife. And then there's Charles Spurgeon, the "prince of preachers." In the course of his decades of ministry, he preached at least ten sermons on Ezekiel 36 alone! Titles include "The Stony Heart Removed" and "Come from the Four Winds, O Breath." During 1859, a year when some would argue he was at his peak, Spurgeon preached three times from Ezekiel: in January on chapter 36, in May on chapter 36 again, and in July on chapter 16.

The question has to be asked, however, when was the last time a typical American evangelical heard a sermon on Ezekiel? In so many ways, like the other prophets, he seems a universe apart from us and our times. And to make matters worse, he is so odd. On the one hand, especially as the later chapters of his book show, his thinking and heart ran deep with grace. If we met him today, we would call him profoundly gospel centered. Think Billy Graham for that side of him. But then add to the Billy Graham piece a full cup of Adrian Monk, the famous detective of recent television fame who is obsessive-compulsive about all the details of life—much like Ezekiel as he describes the intricacies of his wheels within wheels (chap. 1). To Monk and Graham, pour in some of the social activism of a dissident artist like Ai Weiwei. Ezekiel's street drama of laying siege to an engraved stone fits that bill. But still that is not enough, for to it all one must finally slice in some Beethoven: the gifted, tortured, silent soul. Read Ezekiel 3:15.

Very few people would find that mixture of personalities at all appetizing, either in the seventh century BC or today. Ezekiel was indeed odd, as the facts of his life make plain. He spent half of his life in Jerusalem (from birth to around age twenty-five) and half in Babylon (to his death, somewhere around age fifty): a third-culture type, we might call him today. Shortly after he was commissioned as a prophet at age thirty, he was struck dumb, unable to speak for about five years apart from prophetic oracles. Aphasia is how it might be described medically; the biblical text says that God caused

Ezekiel's tongue to cling to the roof of his mouth so that he was mute and unable to reprove the house of Israel, which was not listening anyway and was therefore in rebellion (see Ezek. 3:26). Twice in his Babylonian life he had some sort of out-of-body experience in which he was transported to Jerusalem (Ezek. 8:3; 40:1); for a year and a half he laid siege to a brick (think a large stone block); sometime in his thirties he was forbidden by God to mourn publicly the death of his wife. Strange stuff this, even for a prophet—the kind of stuff that makes for eerie reading. Imagine what it would have been like if you had lived three houses down the street. "Here he comes, that lunatic from another world."

If nothing else, consider this book in your hands an urgent call to move past all these off-putting details and become familiar with a major prophet whose writings have for centuries blessed the people of God. In particular, consider it an invitation to become familiar with four sections of Ezekiel's book that are the peak of his achievement. Four times in his prophetic ministry, Ezekiel was granted "visions from God." His call to prophetic ministry at age thirty was given in the afterglow of the first vision (Ezek. 1:4–28), one in which he saw "the appearance of the likeness of the glory of the Lord" (v. 28). The second, given over a year later at age thirty-one, shocked him with detailed scenes of detestable idolatry, images typical of the abominations being committed in the Jerusalem temple. No wonder, as that vision also revealed, the glory of the Lord was departing—not only from the temple itself but from the most holy city (Ezekiel 8–11). The third vision, the shortest of the four, came after the destruction of the temple by Nebuchadnezzar's armies; Ezekiel was most likely in his forties. In its fourteen verses, God displayed the supernatural power of his breath (or Spirit) to raise back to life a valley of human bodies that had decayed to nothing more than piles of dry bones (Ezek. 37:1–14). The last vision brought Ezekiel, now age fifty, back to Jerusalem, where he saw a new and marvelously altered temple.

From its midst a river spilled out to the east, growing deeper and wider, carrying life and healing in its flow (Ezekiel 40–48).

These visions are not easy to read or understand. And when you place them alongside the other pieces of Ezekiel's book that are peculiar in their own right—things such as forceful condemnations of nations long ago departed, or dramatic enactments performed by Ezekiel in public view—when you pile all these together, you have amassed a mountain of obstacles that stands between you and a meaningful engagement with the Ezekiel text.

The obstacles are real. In fact, for decades every time I neared the end of Jeremiah in my '"through the Bible in a year" reading plan, a dread would descend upon me. I knew that Lamentations was next, a set of dirges that could darken even a Florida sky. And after that, as I knew only too well, loomed Ezekiel. Year after year I could barely make it through the book. And my dislike so intensified over time that at a certain point I felt I was dishonoring the Lord.

"Heavenly Father, this is your Bible, not mine," I would pray. "It is wrong for me to be so negative about one of longest books on your Old Testament read list. It is wrong for me to label it as at best tedious and at worst objectionable." I adapted the prayer at the close of Lamentations (5:21) as an annual cry before starting Ezekiel: "Living God, turn me to Ezekiel so that Ezekiel may turn to me. Open me up to this book so that this book may be opened to me."

God replied. A little answer here, a smaller one there, some insights from an ESV Study Bible,[1] a parenthetic reference to some Ezekiel passage in a book I happened to be reading—over a period of four years God turned my heart. Ezekiel opened up to me. In fact, so complete was the turning that I could hardly wait to get there in my annual Bible reading.

The book of Ezekiel is probably the most underrated book in all of Scripture. For the reasons we have mentioned above along with 153 others, Christians today simply do not read it, know it, or recognize how much they need it. Consider, then, two reasons why the evangelical church needs Ezekiel.

Unimaginable Connections

The first reason we need Ezekiel has to do with the otherwise unimaginable connections between his prophecy and our present cultural moment. Ezekiel tells us right up front that he is writing his prophecy outside the land of Israel. "I was among the exiles by the Chebar canal," he says (Ezek. 1:1) as he prepares us for the first of his visions. His statement is rather like Dorothy Gale's when, dazed by the Technicolor of Oz, she says to her dog, "Toto, I've a feeling we're not in Kansas anymore." Kansas and Oz: Jerusalem and Babylon. To be carried out of the one and dropped into the other is to have every sort of category undone.

For Ezekiel, it all began in 597 BC, at age twenty-five, some five years before his opening vision. Along with several thousand other Jews, he was dragged out of his home, chained to his neighbors, and forced to march one thousand miles to the east. There, in a slave ghetto outside the city of Babylon along one of the city's water sources, the Chebar Canal, he was reduced to making bricks, undoubtedly for one of Nebuchadnezzar's fabulous building projects. Do not think of Ezekiel's bricks as the standard reddish-brown variety used today. They were probably like our construction blocks—large, heavy, and rough.

And they were probably like some other construction blocks, the bricks that Ezekiel's ancestors were forced to make in Egypt alongside a different water source under the cruel whip of a different foreign oppressor. If the accumulated sighs of Ezekiel's fellow exiles recorded in his prophecy are any indication (e.g., Ezek. 33:10), it was not just the destitution, relentless work, hastily built homes, and meager meals that plagued the Jewish people in Babylon. Even deeper was the sense of spiritual despair.

"We were supposed to be the people of the Lord, Yahweh, I AM. He triumphed over Pharaoh and released us from our slavery. So why on God's earth are we here by a Babylonian canal, in bondage under a new Pharaoh, making bricks from mud, living our lives in fear?" Such would have been the whispers of the exiles as they shared with each other their accumulated disbelief, cynicism, and despair (see Ezek. 37:11).

Their situation was previously unimaginable, and it would not be the last time that God's people would find themselves in a similar predicament. In fact, it is this ancient and unimaginable turn of events that connects Ezekiel's prophecy to our cultural moment in the West. Evangelicals in America are facing increasingly unbelievable changes on every front, from curtailments of religious liberty to the redefinition of marriage. Whatever one's political bent, it is hard to believe that a short while ago, in the year 2000, George W. Bush was elected president as a man who claimed an evangelical faith, was openly pro-life, and had campaigned on a platform of "compassionate conservatism." It was a time when Michael Lindsay, now president of Gordon College, could write a book entitled *Faith in the Halls of Power* in which he examined the influence of evangelical Christians at the elite levels of politics, education, the media, and business. How outdated it sounds today! Though superbly researched and written, the former bestseller now sits in Amazon's bargain basement. Yesterday's insiders are today's outsiders, at both the highest levels of cultural influence and down in the streets of the everyday. How times have changed!

Marginalized. Vilified. Laughed at. Misunderstood. Those are the adjectives that many of God's people would choose to describe the sea change, the attitudes they face at work, in school, around town, and across the street. And while we could debate the extent to which the adjectives are accurate to the reality, they are accurate as to the mood—one exactly the same as the cries of Ezekiel's fellow exiles:

"Our bones are dried up, and our hope is lost; we are indeed cut off" (Ezek. 37:11).

How God responded to these cries back in 592 BC, and in particular what the sovereign Lord did with Ezekiel in Babylon, lie behind the second reason why we need Ezekiel today.

Renewed Imaginations

The second reason we need Ezekiel is for divine renewal of that deepest part of our souls, what Christians have traditionally called "imagination." In response to the exiles' cries of despair, God sovereignly moved into Ezekiel's life and gave him, as Ezekiel says, "visions of God" (Ezek. 1:1). Visions. Not an oracle or a burden or a "thus saith the Lord," but visions, things seen—things that, whether "external to Ezekiel's mind or not" (to paraphrase the apostle Paul in 2 Cor. 12:2), would otherwise not have been seen. That is what makes for a biblical vision: apart from God's intervention, it would never have been seen. But God intervened and caught Ezekiel by the imagination, and he saw visions.

Notice that he saw *visions*, plural. The text clearly assigns the plural noun to the opening vision of the wheels within wheels, a vision which, textually speaking, is a carefully constructed single unit of heightened prose and as such a single prophetic experience. The plural noun is Ezekiel's way of communicating the intensity and enormity of the vision. At least for the prophet, it was overwhelming, as were the other three.

So why did God use visions instead of oracles, heightened experience instead of cadenced poetry? The simplest answer is, he did so in order to restore hope. In order to renew and reform the faith of his people in exile, the covenant-loyal God seized Ezekiel by the imagination. Yahweh captured the mind of the son of Buzi with an overpowering, unmediated, sensory presentation of dense truth about (as we shall see) the still-sovereign majesty of the God of Abraham, even though Abraham's descendants were captives in a foreign land. I AM bypassed the rational powers of Ezekiel's mind and went directly for his imagination.

It would be unfair for me to imply that Ezekiel did not have his share of oracles, that is, disclosures of truth that worked through the prophet's reason and verbal capacities. He did, and in all of them (for instance, chaps. 7, 13, 14), what the prophet said is what God said. But with this opening vision, which towers over the rest of the book, what the prophet saw is what God wanted to say, but God said it in visions, in moving images, in real-time video splices of the divine person and authority.

With Ezekiel and the later prophets, the incidence of visions over oracles increases somewhat over that of the earlier prophets. But what is especially noteworthy is how the intensity and abnormality of the visions increase. "Increase" is poor word choice; you could say, the intensity and abnormality "leapfrog." They take an order-of-magnitude jump. The visions of the later prophets, with Ezekiel chief among them, have a bizarre, unnatural, surreal quality. Compare Ezekiel's opening vision of God in chapter 1 to Isaiah's opening vision in the sixth chapter of his book. Here are just a few of the striking contrasts:

Isaiah's Vision (Isaiah 6)	Ezekiel's Vision (Ezekiel 1)
It is set in the temple of the holy city, Jerusalem.	It is set on the plains outside the unholy city, Babylon.
God is high and lifted up; he towers over the temple.	God, gleaming as incandescent metal and flame, appears in human form; he is seated on a sapphire throne above a crystal dome.
God is worshiped by fiery angels called "seraphim."	God is worshiped by unnatural creatures, composites of animal, bird, and human. They are called "cherubim."

Isaiah's Vision (Isaiah 6)	Ezekiel's Vision (Ezekiel 1)
God is stationary; the edge of his robe fills the temple.	God is moving; he is seated on some sort of royal sedan chair.
Recognizable implements of worship appear in the vision: an altar, coals, tongs.	Unrecognizable wheels within wheels take center stage, moving wherever the Spirit directs.

When you compare the two, you cannot help but conclude that they belong in different categories. In terms of the canon of Scripture, Ezekiel definitely has more in common with the book of Revelation than with Isaiah. In fact, the heavenly throne scene in Revelation 4 and 5 parallels Ezekiel's opening vision. And while it would be unwarranted to classify Ezekiel as apocalyptic like Revelation, it is not too far a stretch to see him as the father of apocalyptic.

So strange are Ezekiel's visions that some scholars have post-diagnosed him as a psychological misfit, as someone suffering from a serious psychological disorder. The problem with that approach is that apart from his four visions, the prophet displays a remarkable presence of mind, impeccable rational capacities, and acute powers of observation. Yes, he can sometimes border on the obsessive. Take, for instance, his fixation with describing again and again how the wheels within the wheels rolled in sync with the living creatures (Ezek. 1:15–21). But that sort of over-the-top detailing could simply result from the limits of ancient Hebrew to express what were apparently remarkable wheels.

All in all, it is better to connect the bizarre quality of his visions with the dystopic situation in which he and his contemporaries found themselves. I do not think we can overestimate the impact upon Ezekiel and his contemporaries of the repeated exiles to Babylon, the destruction of the Holy City, and the razing of the Jerusalem temple by pagan armies. Bear with my impossible illustration, but the combined effect of all that would be as if the most outrageous conjectures of the

Jesus Seminar on Christian Origins were proven true, and the New Testament's documents were therefore unreliable. Our faith would be shaken to the core, and we would find ourselves to be, in the words of the apostle Paul, the most pitiful of all people (1 Cor. 15:17–19).

It is hard to imagine a more difficult faith crisis for Old Testament people of God than what Ezekiel and his fellow exiles faced. The combined loss of hope and assurance of divine presence were overwhelming. God's people were in desperate need for something bigger than an oracle. Their thoughts had wandered too far astray to be called back by prophetic logic alone. Instead, they needed to see what they could not see: God's loyal providence. Short of that, they needed to hear someone who himself had seen what they could not see. They needed to hear about the rumbling of the divine chariot rolling across the Babylonian plain. They needed to have one of their own, who had himself been captured, capture their minds with a vision of Yahweh's immense, infinite, unbounded sovereignty—his vast, as I like to call it.

So the Lord went after Ezekiel's imagination, and through him the exiles'. And he did that for strong reason—because human imagination is powerful. It runs deeper than logic and reason—you could almost say that it runs behind them—connecting our rational powers to the emotional and volitional centers of our souls. If you capture someone's imagination, you capture his mind, heart, and will. Do you want a practical demonstration of the validity of that statement? Consider how quickly children identify with the characters in Disney movies. They want to be like them, dress like them, act like them, and sing like them. My wife and I remember one long drive from Princeton to Cape Cod. One of the little girls in the car, a guest, insisted that I play *The Little Mermaid* over and over because she thought she was Ariel. Her imagination was definitely captured; my driving skills were terribly at risk!

The human imagination is where meaning is made, where a vision for life is set, where mind and heart and will converge. It is simultaneously the most strategic and the most forgotten part of the human soul when it comes to Christian discipleship. So Gene and I believe this book is a strategic write, a Christian call to affirm the role of the forgotten part of your mind, your imagination. We do so with the prayer that, as a result, the living God would take our souls captive into the same faith and courage that were Ezekiel's. And, in particular, that he would take us captive into a vivid realization of God (the vision of Ezekiel 1), sin (the vision of Ezekiel 8), hope (the vision of Ezekiel 37), and grace (the vision of Ezekiel 47).

Colloquy

At the beginning of this chapter, we described the imagination as the God-given power of mind to think in pictures, to form a mental image of something not present. We further stated that every one of us uses our imagination day in and day out, in the ordinary stuff of life's flow, whether or not its output would be identified by others as "creative" or "novel" or "imaginative." But as important as they are to this book, these ideas are in service to its bigger points, that we were given this imaginative faculty of mind to glorify God, and it therefore must be redeemed.

When the redeeming God began the first of his two major redemptive moves in biblical history, the exodus, he "saw" the plight of his people in Egypt and thereby "knew" their need for redemption (Ex. 2:25). Similarly for us today, allowing the Lord God to see and know our imaginative capability for what it is constitutes the first step toward *imagination redeemed*. The goal, therefore, of the five colloquy sections of our book is, in prayerful presence before the living God, to develop a fuller personal awareness of our imaginations. For us, that means a number of practical things:

- We want you to recognize that imagination is pervasive in your life.

- We want you to discover where your imagination has both captured faithfully and distorted miserably the glory of God himself.

- We want you to trace out other patterns by which your imagination has been spoiled by sin and captured by the old Adamic self.

- We want to offer you hope and help on how, in and through the risen Christ, the imagination of the "old self" can be displaced by developing and "putting on" the imagination of the "new self" (see Eph. 4:17–24).

As a place to start, consider imagination as a river that runs through all your thinking. Obviously, when you are daydreaming and night dreaming, your imagination is in full flow. But as was stated at the beginning of this chapter, you rely on imagination constantly, not just occasionally. For starters, consider the prevalence of memory. Whenever your mind recalls a face or event or place from the past, it is your imagination at work.[2] The same can be said about things present and things to come. And when we talk of things past, present, and future, we are talking about virtually everything. Your imagination runs through your soul's mental life all the time. To make the point, spend a minute or two thinking through (imagining) these questions:

- What is one of your earliest memories? Bring it to mind. What scene do you see? What faces? Do you hear any words? What are they? What feelings do you feel?

- Picture in your mind the closest intersection to your home. What do you see and hear? Is there a traffic light? Is the intersection busy? Are the turns sharp and difficult?

- Imagine (with apologies to Steven Covey's *Seven Habits of Highly Effective People*) the scene at your funeral. Who is there? What songs are sung? What texts are read? Is a sermon preached?

About what and by whom? What is said about you? And how does all this make you feel today?

Let's take this imagination audit a step further. Draw to mind something that you have been worrying about recently. What is it? How does imagination play a part in it, specifically, what possible scene in the future do you envision as the reason for your worry? And speaking about the future, what are you looking forward to? What picture do you attach to it? As I, Matt, write this, I am sitting in my home in Princeton with mounds of snow outside. It is the winter of 2014, and every third day over the past two weeks we have had bitter cold storms pile snow upon snow upon snow. My heart is at once filled with pain and joy: pain at the thought (picture) of taking shovel in hand once again to clear the driveway, joy at knowing (picturing) that, Lord willing, during the first week of August I will be kneeling on the sand of the Jersey Shore scooping out a tunnel with my granddaughter, Eden.

The point of this exercise is not to develop some sort of New Age consciousness. It is instead to become a better steward of the imaginative capacity that God has given to you. And a major piece of that stewardship is to identify the pervasiveness of imagination in the big and little of your soul's daily flow.

Oh, Lord, we are truly fearfully and wonderfully made. Thank you for this power you have given us to imagine. We offer our imaginations to you as a living sacrifice. Help us to discern how we misuse this gift, how it is fallen, how we indulge in sinful and idolatrous imaginings. We ask that you redeem our imaginations and make them holy. Bless the venture of reading this book. Please use it, by the power of your Word, for our good and for your glory. In the name of Jesus, who has redeemed every facet of our lives by his blood, we pray. Amen.

2

Imagination and God

Such was the appearance of the likeness
of the glory of the LORD.

Ezekiel 1:28

Beauty will save the world.

Fyodor Dostoevsky

From Gene

We cannot imagine God in his fullness. He is too vast and so far transcends us that we can never get him into our little heads. Just as we cannot fully comprehend him with our intellects, we cannot fully capture him in our imaginations.

To be sure, we can make up deities with our imaginations, ones that completely make sense to our limited understanding, but those are false gods. Not only do they not exist; they are *idols*, a term that derives from the Greek word for "image." We can imagine a god we would like to worship and then craft a graven image to give it an external existence. Even if we don't take that step, even if our deity remains just a mental image—as in deism, Unitarianism, or Islam— we still commit idolatry if we worship the product of our or someone else's imagination.

33

Even Ezekiel, as Matt will discuss later in this chapter, when given a "vision" of spiritual reality, was not shown a direct sensory manifestation of God. He was shown "the appearance of the likeness of the glory of the Lord" (Ezek. 1:28). Not God, but the glory of God. Not the full glory of God—that would surely have incinerated Ezekiel like a fly in a nuclear reactor—but the likeness of his glory. And not just the likeness, which Ezekiel still probably had no frame of reference for, but "the appearance of the likeness."

Thus God does accommodate us minuscule creatures with our feeble imaginations and our primitive intellects. He gives us appearances and likenesses that we can use to think about him. The Bible is full of them—Father, King, potter, shepherd, bridegroom, and on and on, on virtually every page. Our minds being what they are, we cannot help but picture something of God in our minds when we think about him or address him in prayer. Picturing God as a bright, pulsating light may seem more spiritual, but it is just as figurative as picturing him as a benevolent man with a long, white beard. We can never "capture" the Holy One of Israel in our minds. He is always far more. And we dare not try to reduce him or recast him according to our desires. But God reveals himself to us. He himself gives us the ways he wants us to think about him.

Specifically, he communicates himself to us by means of his Word. The difference between idolatry and apprehension of the true God is the difference between a humanly or self-devised mental construction and hearing the voice of God, who reveals himself to us by means of human language. If we are to conceive of him correctly—whether in our understanding, our imagination, or our will—our minds must be saturated with Holy Scripture.

This point is so important that we should linger on it for a while. When I was trying to explain this project to a pastor friend of mine, he said, "That sounds Eastern." Emphasizing the role of the imagination in the spiritual life smacked to him of the use of icons, a word that literally means "image," the ostensibly sacred pictures of Christ and the saints that the Eastern Orthodox meditate upon in prayer and devotion. "No," I told him, "this book has nothing to do with icons." Imagination is the source of art, and we'll get to that later in the book, but forming a mental image in response to language is very different from responding to a visual object. Nor is this book about the controversies over the use of art in worship. The two of us authors, I being Lutheran and Matt being Reformed, would have some disagreements on that issue, but that is not what this book is about. This is primarily a book about Bible reading: more specifically, making the connection between Scripture and the imagination.

While we are at it, I might add that this book is not offering commentary on how visual images in today's culture are displacing language, nor is its silence on that subject suggesting that there is nothing wrong with that. Elsewhere I have made the case that allowing the visual images of computer and video screens (with the mind-set that goes with them) to take the place of words and the Word of God (with the mind-set that goes with them) can erode a vital Christian faith.[1]

Instead, this book is specifically about language and the kind of thinking that language evokes. We are talking about words, not pictures; mental images, not graven images. Our "icon"—the sacred object that connects us spiritually to the divine—is the Word of God. And that Word of God creates images in the minds of its readers and hearers.

Though we cannot fully imagine God, he imagined us. In creating the universe, God made tangible, material, concrete realities, which we can apprehend with our senses. Among the things he created were human beings. Not only that, he created each individual human being who ever lived or who will live, including you and me. As Matt will show later in the chapter, before we even existed—indeed, before the universe even existed, "before the foundation of the world"—God imagined us, chose us, and resolved to save us (Eph. 1:4).

And, astoundingly, in the course of his creation of men and women, God imagined himself:

> Then God said, "Let us make man in our image, after our likeness. And let them have dominion over the fish of the sea and over the birds of the heavens and over the livestock and over all the earth and over every creeping thing that creeps on the earth." So God created man in his own image, in the image of God he created him; male and female he created them. (Gen. 1:26–27)

Such is the status of human beings in God's creation! God made us in *his* image. This is the source of our human powers—to think, to feel, to will, and to imagine—the "likeness" we have with God.

But then we sinned, and in our fallen condition the image of God was effaced. We retain a certain likeness to our Creator in our powers and in the sacred value of every human life (Gen. 9:6). But we no longer share his holiness, perfection, and goodness.

To fully restore his image in us, God the Father did something even more astounding than his creation of the universe. His true image in the depths of his Godhood is his Son. " He is the image of the invisible God," writes the apostle Paul (Col. 1:15). Furthermore, the Son is the very imagination of God, the model, the agent, and the purpose of all creation.

> For by him all things were created, in heaven and on earth, visible and invisible, whether thrones or dominions or rulers or authorities—all things were created through him and for him. And he is before all things, and in him all things hold together. (Col. 1:16–17)

> The Word became flesh and dwelt among us (John 1:14).

Jesus Christ is the ultimate self-expression of the Father, a physical, tangible, material, bodily manifestation of God himself. And through his life of holiness, perfection, and goodness; his sin-bearing; his atoning death; and his resurrection from the dead, we are reconciled to God, and his image—Christ's image—is restored in us:

> You have put off the old self with its practices and have put on the new self, which is being renewed in knowledge after the image of its creator. (Col. 3:9–10)

> And we all, with unveiled face, beholding the glory of the Lord, are being transformed into the same image from one degree of glory to another. (2 Cor. 3:18)

Imagination and the Theologians

The imagination of God is the source of the imagination of human beings. The connection between them was first explored by Augustine. The Trinity, he said, is reflected in human beings, who were created in his image. Augustine saw a trace of the triune nature of God in the three faculties of the human mind, which he identified as the understanding, the will, and the memory. Memory, as he saw it, embraces what we are calling the imagination; it is the capacity to conjure up mental images of the lived past. Ancient and medieval thinkers considered memory to be the primary category in our ability to picture images in our minds, since we could never imagine a tree unless we remembered what a tree looks like, and we could never imagine events in the future unless we recalled knowledge and experiences from the past. In his treatise *On the Trinity*, Augustine explores the interrelationships between memory, understanding, and the will, seeing them as analogous to the interrelationships between the persons of the Trinity (Father, Son, and Holy Spirit, respectively). He concludes his discussion with the following summary:

> We have reasoned also from the creature which God made, and, as far as we could, have warned those who demand a reason on such subjects to behold and understand His invisible things, so

far as they could, by those things which are made and especially by the rational or intellectual creature which is made after the image of God; through which glass, so to say, they might discern as far as they could, if they could, the Trinity which is God, in our own memory, understanding, will. Which three things, if any one intelligently regards as by nature divinely appointed in his own mind, and remembers by memory, contemplates by understanding, embraces by love how great a thing that is in the mind, whereby even the eternal and unchangeable nature can be recollected, beheld, desired, doubtless that man finds an image of that highest Trinity. And he ought to refer the whole of his life to the remembering, seeing, loving that highest Trinity, in order that he may recollect, contemplate, be delighted by it.[2]

Thomas Aquinas would spin off imagination from memory, turning it into the faculty for thinking in terms of sense perceptions. This included fantasy (*phantasia*), the ability to conceive sensory images apart from their existence in the actual world: "For the retention and preservation of these [sensory] forms, the 'phantasy' or 'imagination' is appointed; which are the same, for phantasy or imagination is as it were a storehouse of forms received through the senses."[3]

But it is Luther who writes about imagination in connection with the Word of God. He does so in his treatise *Against the Heavenly Prophets* (1525), written in response to Andreas Karlstadt, the leader of iconoclastic riots that broke out in Wittenberg while the Reformer was in hiding at Wartburg Castle. Luther defends Christian works of art by relating them to the "mental images" that automatically form in our minds when we read or hear the Word of God:

Of this I am certain, that God desires to have his works heard and read, especially the passion of our Lord. But it is impossible for me to hear and bear it in mind without forming mental images of it in my heart. For whether I will or not, when I hear of Christ, an image of a man hanging on a cross takes form in my heart, just as the reflection of my face naturally appears in the water when I look into it.[4]

Luther goes on to say, "If it is not a sin but good to have the image of Christ in my heart, why should it be a sin to have it in my eyes?"[5] On that point, of course, other Protestant theologians would differ. But Luther here is describing the imagination as primarily an interior, mental faculty that functions "whether I will or not" in response to language—specifically, to the language of God, which is given to us in the Bible.

Meanwhile, on the Roman Catholic side, Ignatius of Loyola, the founder of the Jesuit order, was adapting the Augustinian psychology—memory, understanding, will—along with a Thomist awareness of the imagination, in his *Spiritual Exercises*. These outlined a technique for Christian meditation, in which the meditator would first vividly imagine a scene from the life of Christ ("the composition of place," engaging the memory); then reflect on its meaning (the "analysis," engaging the understanding); then pray to Christ in love (the "colloquy," engaging the will).

Ignatius's composition of place involved imagining the scene—things such as the baby Jesus in the manger, our Lord's crucifixion—by systematically engaging each of the five senses. What would it look like? What would I hear (the lowing of the animals, the curses of the soldiers)? What would I smell (the manure of the animals, sweat and blood)? What would be the tastes in the scene (the baby's milk, the vinegary wine)? What could be touched (e.g., the texture of the hay, the sharpness of the metal nails, the splinters of the wood). Forming such a vivid imaginative conception caused the meditator to be intimately and personally involved in the biblical narrative, giving the analysis an intensely personal application ("Why did Christ undergo this? For me?") and giving the colloquy a passionate force ("Oh, Christ child, give me your innocence!" "Crucified Lord, I praise you for bearing my sins!").

To be sure, the Protestants opposed the notion that the elaborate "spiritual exercises" were good works that granted spiritual merit. They also opposed the mysticism that often accompanied these meditations. They certainly opposed the Jesuits and their counter-Reformation piety. And yet, as Louis L. Martz has documented in his book *The Poetry of Meditation*,[6] Ignatian meditation as a way to contemplate Scripture was widely adopted by Protestants, including the Puritans. Martz quotes a number of Puritan meditations that follow the three-part structure of composition (imagination)/analysis (understanding)/colloquy (will) with great precision.

The main purpose of Martz's book is to show how this kind of meditation has influenced Christian poetry. For example, the Protestant John Donne (who had a Jesuit education) writes, "Mark in my heart, O soul, where thou dost dwell / The picture of Christ crucified."[7] Then follows a vivid multisensory description of Christ on the cross:

Tears in His eyes quench the amazing light,
Blood fills his frowns, which from His pierced head fell,
And can that tongue adjudge thee unto hell,
Which pray'd forgiveness for His foes' fierce spite?[8]

This imaginative composition becomes the foundation for Donne's analysis, which follows: he need not fear death and judgment ("What if this present were the world's last night?"),[9] because Jesus has suffered and died for him. This, in turn, inspires a colloquy—in this case with his troubled soul—that orients his will to the love of Christ: "So I say to thee / . . . This beauteous form assures a piteous mind."[10]

To summarize: when we read, whether a poem or a novel or the Bible, we are conjuring up the images ourselves, in our own minds, as inspired by the words the author uses. This is different from seeing a work of art—whether a painting, a movie, or a YouTube video—in which the image is outside ourselves and was made by someone else.

The visual image and the mental image are related to each other, imagination being foundational to them both, but they are not the same. Both can be problematic for sinful, fallen human beings.

But the imagination is a gift of God, and it finds its fullest expression in God. His imagination led to his creation. His imagination was manifested in his image, in us human beings and supremely in Christ. And God reveals himself and restores his image in us through Christ by means of his Word. That Word addresses our understanding, our will, and our imagination. When we attend closely to the words of the Bible and imagine what they are saying in a fuller way, we become more intimately and personally involved in Scripture, and the Word of God has a greater impact on us. To demonstrate that, let us turn to Matt and the book of Ezekiel.

From Matt

Indulge me for a moment as I think through some thoughts theological about imagination and the Godhead. Let's start with Genesis. In the beginning, God created. But before the beginning, he imagined. Before speaking into existence the heavens and the earth, the eternal three-in-one, Father, Son, and Spirit, sketched a plan of creation, fall, and redemption and immediately colored in the specifics: the who, the how, the when, the where, the means, the people, their times, their places, their names, their days, their faces. All this was pictured in the Eternal's mind before he began to create.

That's why the apostle Paul writes of the Ephesian believers' being chosen in Christ "before the foundation of the world" (Eph. 1:4)— chosen in God's mind at some point between his conceiving the creation-redemption plan and his inaugurating it with the words, "Let there be light" (Gen. 1:4). They were chosen not as faceless entities or empty ciphers but as named individuals whose lives would be lived in specific times and actual places. In this regard note how John speaks of "the book of life" from "before the foundation of the world" in which was written the names of those who would belong to the Lamb (Rev. 13:8). Names: individualized persons who had already been differentiated—may I say imagined—in the mind of God. Do you see? God did not paint with a broad brush when he set the salvation plan within the Trinity long before anything had been spoken into being. No, there were details to it, imagined specifics that would be actual when the fullness of time arrived. And those details included the names and faces of those chosen to be in Christ *as well as, even more strikingly*, the specifics of Christ's work of redemption. That is why Peter affirms that the Christ was as a flawless lamb whose death was "foreknown before the foundation of the world" (1 Pet. 1:20).

Consider all this in relation to one such person, one such "name," Matt Ristuccia. When I was at seminary, I did what so many others had carelessly done before me. I overzealously reduced divine foreknowledge to a series of rational choices in a masterful piece of logic. It happened during one of my favorite courses, second-year theology. The focus that year was on God's work of salvation, and a whole unit was devoted to the order of divine decrees. Essential issues were covered, and as a result I figured out where I stood in the lapsarian and electionist debates. But for me and many of my peers, the net effect of the study *in relation to the person of God* was to reduce him to the master of crisp syllogism and sequential logic: first he made this decree, then that one, then the one over there, and finally the one left standing. The farthest thing from my mind was any sense that God's rational powers existed simultaneously and indistinguishably alongside what at the human level we call "imagination." And how I missed out! For what in the godhead is fused into a single and simple whole, God's rational *and* imaginative powers, were unavoidably pulled apart in my human understanding. And his imagination got lost in the process.

But, in fact, divine reason and imagination exist and interfuse each other much like hydrogen and oxygen are bound together in pure, clear water. The two simultaneously and mutually inter-dwell. What this means is that the Creator of the universe is master of both its physics and its beauty. He alone brought into existence, say, *both* mathematics with all its precise rules and impeccable sequences *and* colors with all their evocative shades and tones and combinations. To him be the praise for all of it!

What I said in chapter 1 should therefore not be surprising: specifically, that when God called Ezekiel to serve as prophet to the Babylonian exiles, he didn't give him simply a series of closely argued oracles. For sure, he would do so at later points in the prophet's ministry. Ezekiel 33:1–9 is a case in point. The unit consists of a series of well-pleaded oral arguments, almost courtroom in their intensity, based on the concept of prophet as watchman. With a text like that, no one could argue that reason does not have its place in the prophet's writings. But as a way to capture the whole of Ezekiel's heart and thereby motivate him into the arduous ministry of speaking to "nations of rebels," a "rebellious house" (Ezek. 2:3, 5), God provided Ezekiel with *visions*: vivid pictures in a vivid sequence—better, an extended and intense video clip—of things Ezekiel could not otherwise see. God engaged Ezekiel's imagination so that he saw and recorded one of the most overwhelming visions of God to be found in Holy Scripture. So it is fitting for us to turn to this, the first of Ezekiel's visions, in order to understand it in its own right and then through it to think more closely about the role of imagination in relation to God.

A Vision of Visions

Ezekiel's first vision, the most awe-inspiring portion of which is found in the first chapter of his book, had an enormous effect on the prophet himself. It caused him to fall to the ground in fear (1:28), provided the basis for his call (chaps. 2 and 3), and left him mute (3:26). Since Ezekiel's time, the vision has had an incomparably powerful impact on others. A branch of mystical Judaism known as *merkabah* is so named because it grew out of Ezekiel's opening vision; its adherents developed their disciplines and aspirations out of meditation upon the text, in particular the wheeled chariots (Heb. *merkabah*) that rolled as one with the Spirit. Interestingly, at least one New Testament scholar, no less than N. T. Wright, has proposed that Saul (to become the apostle Paul) had been meditating in the *merkabah* tradition at the time of his conversion.[11]

Whether these claims about Paul are true or not, God only knows. But it is clear that as a result of this vision and its accompanying call, Ezekiel himself became someone with an all-controlling passion to know God. A. W. Tozer once wrote of the "difference between a scribe who has read and a prophet who has seen" the Lord.[12] Ezekiel falls into the latter category, and he does so because of a captured imagination. How that happened is something that began on a hot and humid July afternoon in 593 BC. So to that event let us now turn our attention and, in particular, to three phrases that help unlock its mysteries.

Begin at the End: Begin with God

The best place to begin understanding Ezekiel's inaugural vision is at its conclusion, with the prophet's summary: "Such was the appearance of the likeness of the glory of the Lord. And when I saw it, I fell on my face, and I heard the voice of one speaking" (1:28). It is a rather obvious point, but behind all the layers of appearance and likeness, Ezekiel caught a glimpse, maybe I should say a gaze, of God himself. As confused and overwhelmed as the prophet was, there was no question in his mind as to what he had seen: Ezekiel's first vision was one "of the glory of the Lord."

Let me rephrase that. In order to initiate a work of restoration among the Babylonian exiles, the Lord presented Ezekiel with a direct, unmediated vision of his own unmatchable glory. God started with a theological vision. God started with himself, which is a rather obvious point, to be sure, but one not to be skipped over. Step back and you will see what I mean. Ezekiel and his fellow Jews are out of the land, they are reliving the Egyptian oppression, they wonder if God is out there, and they fear the worst: that God either has abandoned them or was never a reality to begin with. Meanwhile, so bitter is their cynicism that, as some have argued, the role of prophet itself is under attack, which in turn leads to further disillusionment with God himself.[13] So where does the Lord start in restoring hope? He does not start with a political vision of a restored Jerusalem (he will do that later on). He does not start with a sociological vision of the human condition or the devastations of sin in sixth-century Judea (again, he will do that later on). He does not start with an artistic vision of the *shalom* that will take place once Babylon has been defeated, or even a dream-like vision of divine power to restore (again, he will do that later on). Rather, the Lord recaptures his people with a vision of himself.

People need a robust vision of God. He alone is the starting point for a vigorous Christian imagination. What we believe about God—deep down inside what we imagine him to be—is the control lever of the human soul and the believer's life. It is not enough for us to be able to affirm right truths about God. The truths have to go deeper so as to reform what we fundamentally understand and conceive God to be.

It is not uncommon for people who profess an orthodox faith in great gospel truths such as the person of Christ, the Trinity, salvation by faith alone, the absolute authority of Scripture, and the bodily death and resurrection to all the while hold underneath a deeply flawed picture of what God is like. I have seen this time and again in my decades of pastoral ministry. Josh is a case in point. An accomplished graduate of Princeton University, he went on to earn his MDiv and DMin degrees at premier evangelical seminaries. He knows the Scripture like the back of his hand, he is a recognized leader in his local church, he is happily married, and yet, when he recently met with me, he confessed that to this day he struggles with a deep suspicion of God.

"Father?" he shot back, when I asked him if he thought of God in this way. "It is *so* hard for me to think of God as a father. Maybe I do in my better moments, when the Spirit has me in his flow. But down underneath all the layers of my teaching and leading is a picture of God as a cruel tyrant, and it is a picture that keeps on surfacing. It bobs up like a beach ball that you try to hold down under the waves. I can't help it. It just bounces up. Most of the time, way down inside, I fear God as an unyielding taskmaster, the 'hard man' of the parable of the talents." Josh's reference was to Matthew 25:24.

Josh is like all of us; he bears in his person the consequence of sin. He is an example of what you might call a "dissociation of sensibility."[14] The pieces of our soul that were originally created to work in unison have been torn asunder (dissociated) by sin. So our feelings are cut off from our rational powers, and our rational powers are cut off from our will, and our will is cut off from our affections, and our affections are cut off from our imagination, and so the interrupting circle goes on and on. We are in a terribly discordant mess, as cacophonous within ourselves as a gathered symphony, each instrument playing its own melody in its own key.

But Christ came to rescue. In him we see who God actually is: "Whoever has seen me has seen the Father" (John 14:9). And in him we see humanity as it should be, humanity as we will one day be in the age to come. With him there is the wonder of associated sensibilities. His feelings and will and mind and imagination all worked in unison. What he did, he did 100 percent out of deep affection and love for the Father. What he believed, he felt.[15] Even in the darkest moment of his earthly struggle, when in Gethsemane he asked the Father to take the cup from him, there was still a deeper resolve, a settled rest, to do the Father's will and not his own.

This is where the Spirit, the sanctifier of God's people, is taking all who trust in Christ. And one of the Spirit's main works of grace is to reform that deeply held picture of God that sits beneath our mind's more conscious workings. So, I argue, that is why God began his renewing work with Ezekiel by giving him a vision of the Lord himself. Ezekiel, like the rest of us, had an imagined picture of God that needed to be transformed. And so, as we shall see, it was.

But before we examine the actual specifics of that transformation, let me probe your heart with unavoidable questions: How do you imagine God? What is your underlying vision of God? Do you imagine him along the lines of Josh's god, a cruel and heartless taskmaster? Or is it more like the prevailing American view of moralistic therapeutic deism, a distant god who exists in order to empower us to become everything we would like to be as long as we do good and help the people around us? Or is it more along the lines of the smiling and benign deity claimed by one in four Americans, a benevolent god who is very involved in helping the people of this world, who does not feel anger toward evildoers and would certainly never judge anyone?[16]

What is your underlying vision of God? Where does your theological imagination lean?

Three Degrees of Separation

A second phrase that is important for our understanding Ezekiel's vision is also found in verse 28: "the appearance of the likeness of the glory of the Lord." The phrase is a buffered statement, one that simultaneously connects and distances. Let me explain.

The difficulties of Ezekiel's first vision are evident and many. Think of a scale, a Scripture-understandability scale with a range of one to ten, where one refers to a text that is open and accessible to all, and ten refers to a text that is impenetrable and seemingly sealed shut. So, as examples, we will assign John 11:35, "Jesus wept," a value of one: perspicuous, clear, easy to comprehend. At the other end of the scale we will place Revelation 13:18, in which the author calculates the number of the beast, and "his number is 666." The text is intentionally obscure, impenetrable, an enigma worthy of the Sphinx. So where on this scale of one to ten do we place Ezekiel's first vision? Three? Seven and a half? Nine? Honestly, if it were my decision, I would place it at fifty-eight.

The vision is off the charts. Early-century rabbis had rules about who could study this text, when, and with whom. Later, the master of Reformed exegesis, John Calvin, wrote that its "vision is obscure, and I do not understand it." So strangely esoteric are the details of the vision that it became a cultural phenomenon in the American seventies. In books such as *The Chariot of the Gods*, author Erich von Daniken and thousands of followers interpreted Ezekiel 1 as an ancient record of an encounter with aliens from outer space.

Ezekiel's text will not allow psychedelic seventies' nonsense. Nevertheless, it seems that Ezekiel himself did not fully understand what he saw. He describes the vision as "the appearance of the likeness of the glory of the LORD." In other words, the vision was "sort of like the sort of like the visual sort of like God." Count the "sort of likes." There are three. That is, three degrees of separation: if you start with God, there is first of all his glory (the one-step-removed visual representation of who he is), which is then represented in a "likeness," which is further distanced outward by its "appearance."

These multiple degrees of separation contain in themselves a significant revelation of God; in particular, they point to the mysterious aspect of his transcendence. God is incomprehensible and cloaked, and for our own good. I do not mean to suggest that we humans cannot know about God or even know God. We can—through Christ and his Scriptures. But we can never fully know or comprehend God. He is as understandable to us in his fullness as the Empire State Building is to a cockroach that lives in an inside wall of its basement. And the moment we think we have figured out God or comprehended his fullness, at that moment we have deceived ourselves. If nothing else, at that point our imagination needs the bracing vision of Ezekiel 1.

One of the strengths of imagination over the mind's power of discursive reason is its ability to behold, see, and let stand. The imagination does not in itself press us to figure something out. Take, as an example, a dream. It is often the case that a dream can be remembered (imagined) for the first few minutes after we wake up. In those moments of reliving it, we can see its images and feel its emotional impact, and all the while another part of our mind might be trying to figure it out. Reason, in other words, is sitting alongside imagination, trying to draw from it some sort of meaning. Whether the dream has a meaning is hardly the point. Instead, what I am saying is that it is not your imagination that is demanding the explanation. It is your reason. The imagination itself is content with the not knowing.

Negative Capability: Imagination and Faith

This not-knowing aspect of our imagination can be called a "negative capability," and it is of great value to our faith.[17] There is a positive capability of faith: its ability to take hold of a promise, to pray through a trial, to apply a text to a life situation. It is mostly these positive capabilities that we have in mind when we talk about growing our faith. But as with our imagination, so with our faith: there is a negative capability to be recognized and appreciated. Faith's negative capability is engaged when we are willing to *not* understand, *not* do something, *not* explain, *not* act, *not* challenge or doubt or complain. Like the weaned child in Psalm 131, we are content to sit in the lap of God and not demand anything—except God's presence itself.

It is with such an attitude of reverent submission to the fearsome unknowability of God that the prophet Ezekiel falls on his face. So, too, our faith needs the sanctifying reverence of imagination's negative capability. By it we are able to trust God in the presence of unexplained mysteries. One of my favorite examples of this is Sarah Edwards, the should-be-famous wife of her much more famous husband, Jonathan. Lamenting his abrupt death at age fifty-four, she wrote to their daughter:

> What shall I say. A holy and good God has covered us with a dark cloud. O that we may all kiss the rod and lay our hands on our mouths. The Lord has done it. He has made me adore His goodness that we had him so long. But my God lives and He has my heart. O what a legacy my husband and your father has left us. We are all given to God and there I am and love to be.[18]

Sarah's appeal to faithful surrender in the middle of the hard disciplines of God ("the rod") rests squarely upon the imagination's negative capability, so vividly expressed with the phrase "lay our hands on our mouths." There is nothing we can say. There is no further question we should ask. This trial is from a holy and good God, and in his goodness we can rest without knowing all his purposes.

Perhaps, though, I write too much about the negative capability of the sanctified imagination. Ezekiel may not have understood a lot about the vision of chapter 1, but he did understand some things. And it is to these that we now turn.

The Lord God of Always and Everywhere

The third phrase that offers a key to Ezekiel's vision is again found in 1:28, where Ezekiel tells us that he saw "the glory of the Lord." In spite of its staggering incomprehensibilities, the vision had enough coherence that Ezekiel took away some truths about God himself, for God revealed himself in it. The million-dollar question, of course, is what exactly did God reveal about himself? Let's take that in two steps.

First, let me help you make sense of the structure of the vision, for, believe it or not, there is one here.[19] All that Ezekiel saw was arranged in layers, three to be precise. First, in mid-air we have the four living creatures. The creatures appear to be Ezekiel's version of the Babylonian *sirrush*, a composite creature that has been unearthed in various archaeological digs. The *sirrush* was a combination of creatures, each one the highest from four realms of ancient cosmology: the realms of humans, wild animals, domesticated animals, and birds. Ezekiel's creatures, which he later identifies as seraphim (10:1), are composed from these four realms. Each one has the face of a man, a lion, an ox, and an eagle (1:10). The seraphim are therefore powerfully fearsome creatures, high above the created realm in all aspects. But they are nevertheless as inferior to the Lord as any courtroom servant of the time was to the king served. The point is, the Lord is so much more intelligent than a man, so much more ferocious than a lion, so much stronger than an ox, so much swifter than an eagle. Babylon, beware! Exiles, take heart!

But there is more. Babylonian *sirrush* were often carved in the entrance gates of palaces, presumably acting as gatekeeper or protector. Similarly, the seraphim are guardians of any access (or vision of) God's holiness. In particular, here in Ezekiel they seem to be the bearers and protectors of a portable throne or sedan chair upon which sits the almighty King. That is why there is movement in the vision; the King's throne travels toward Ezekiel. It comes "out of the north" (1:4)—that is, from the direction one would travel if coming from Jerusalem, across and down the arc of the Euphrates basin. Zion's King is arriving in Babylon! And the seraphim are there to serve him in his journey. So again, Babylon, beware.

As I have said, the vision is layered. Below the seraphim lies a bottom layer. It consists of the wheels, so exactingly described by Ezekiel in verses 15 through 21. The wheels clearly have an "unrestricted freedom of movement";[20] as directed by the wind/Spirit/breath (the

Hebrew word *ruah*, as in the valley of the bones in Ezekiel 37), they move on the face of the earth as the seraphim move through the air. This correspondence of movement between layers, all directed by the wind/Spirit/breath of the Lord, is a central detail for Ezekiel and, as we will see, points us clearly toward one of the main meanings of the vision.

Above the seraphim is the highest of the vision's three layers, distinctly set off from the other two by some sort of glass dome that stretches across the sky. Ezekiel refers to this vast dome as "an expanse, shining like awe-inspiring crystal" (v. 22). The dome is transparent, which is why Ezekiel can talk about what lies above it. And as strange as the dome itself may be, even more strange is what lies on top of it: "Above the expanse . . . was the likeness of a throne . . . and seated above the likeness of a throne was a likeness with a human appearance" (v. 26). The text goes on to describe this human appearance as both fiery and glowing like metal. It is, of course, the Lord himself whom Ezekiel is seeing, the Lord God as a theophany, a preincarnation glimpse of God in human likeness. And wonder of wonders, he is not seated in the Jerusalem temple; instead, he is seated high above the plains outside Babylon.

If we place the three-storied structure of Ezekiel 1 alongside a different scene in Scripture, the meaning of Ezekiel's opening vision emerges. The theophany in Ezekiel's vision is seated above a transparent crystal expanse, a detail that is very much reminiscent of the Lord's appearance to Moses, Aaron, his sons, and the seventy elders of Israel on Mount Sinai. In Exodus 24:9–10 it is recorded that they "saw the God of Israel. There was under his feet as it were a pavement of sapphire stone, like the very heaven for clearness." For Moses and company, the divine vision came immediately after the receiving of the Ten Commandments and its appendices, the "Book of the Covenant" (Ex. 20:19–23:33). For Ezekiel, the vision comes immediately before his call to prophetic ministry (Ezekiel 2–3), a ministry in which he will act as a latter-day Moses. As we will see in a later chapter, much like Moses, Ezekiel will provide a plan for a new temple, consecrate a new altar, and establish new sacrifices.

Ezekiel and Moses. Both were allowed to see the glory of the sovereign judge. In the case of Moses, he was seen directly; in the case of Ezekiel, in a vision. But for both, the glory was of the holy and sovereign judge, who sits above the earth, who gives supreme decrees, who orders the paths of his people, judges their enemies, and establishes a foundation for a distinctive culture.

The difference, of course, is that Moses sees God on the holy mountain, Mount Sinai, while Ezekiel sees God over the plains of Babylon, a city in opposition to God, Babel, the eventual harlot of Revelation. But God is still seated over the anti-city, and his decrees and power are still operating down on the face of the earth through all the layers of wind/spirit and creatures and wheels turning. Ezekiel's vision, in other words, is about a God who, by means of his providence, is just as much the warrior God as was the God of Moses. The Lord is just as much in control of the events of the world, even in God-forsaken Babylon, as he was at Mount Sinai and the Red Sea.

The great American Puritan pastor, Cotton Mather, captured the essence of Ezekiel's vision well in a series of eight thesis statements that reflected upon different aspects of the vision in light of the new covenant. I will mention two. First, concerning the throne above the crystal dome with the likeness of a man seated upon it, Mather wrote: "It is the glorious Lord Jesus Christ upon the throne by whom all the changes of the world are ordered and managed." The vision reminds us today that Christ is the king of providence. A second thesis is based upon the wheels, which are four in number, with four capturing the corners or quarters of the world: "All the quarters and all the ages of the world have all their changes governed by the Lord, whose kingdom ruleth over all."[21] In other words, Christ the king of providence is sovereign over all workings in all places at all times in, with, and through all people: layers of workings underneath the divine throne, wheels within wheels moving where the Spirit takes them. As the apostle Paul put it, Christ is "before all things, and in him all things hold together" (Col. 1:17).

Colloquy

The Lord saw to it that Ezekiel had a fresh vision of the divine glory in preparation for a challenging call. The Lord captured Ezekiel's imagination with himself. And so it goes with us. The critical step toward redeeming one's imagination is to fill it with God himself. And to that end, an intentional response and a prayer now follow.

Various suggestions are made as to how a Christian might fill his or her imagination with God and his glory. For those in the Orthodox tradition, icons are recommended as guides for the imagination to apprehend and worship God. Roman Catholics take an even more material, if not at times physical and corporeal, route: the practice of pilgrimages, moving through the stations of the cross, and other disciplines that purport to bring together the physical and the spiritual.

We propose a much more sober and scriptural method, that of biblical meditation. Unlike so many different types of meditation offered in our day and age, biblical meditation has a distinct focus that sets it apart from all the others. As the author of Psalm 1 writes, the blessed person meditates upon *the law of the Lord* day and night (v. 2). Biblical meditation takes the texts of Scripture as its food and fuel. Working with the very words of Scripture, biblical meditation encourages the disciple to ask questions of the text in order to unlock and "talk oneself through" its meaning.[22] And as is often the case with a true discipline practiced in response to God's grace, the intentionally limiting focus (in this case, meditating upon Scripture alone) leads to a surprising end: the serendipitous freeing of the soul in true worship (in this case, knowing and loving the three-in-one God more).

I (Gene) already explained in chapter 1 a simple three-part model for biblical meditation. It is a tried and true model. I say that because it was used by Jesuits and Puritans, the great seventeenth-century Christian poets and American colonists writing in their journals.[23] What follows is a summary of its three parts:

- *Composition of place.* Reading a passage from scripture and vividly picturing it in your mind, paying close attention to the Bible's descriptions and figures of speech.

- *Analysis.* Thinking about that passage and reflecting upon what it means.

- *Colloquy.* Applying the passage to your own life, leading to personal conviction, resolution, and prayer.

Classical Christian educators will see in this pattern that of the *trivium*—a movement from grammar (getting the material fixed in your mind) to logic (thinking deeply about it) to rhetoric (expressing a personal insight or application). Just as the *trivium* reflects how the human mind learns any subject in a comprehensive way, this tripartite meditation on the Bible helps us toward an in-depth confrontation with God's Word, engaging all of our mental powers (the imagination, the intellect, and the will).

There are, of course, other models that one can follow in learning to meditate upon God's Word. Our goal here is not to repeat what others have taught regarding this important Christian discipline.[24] Rather, what we want to emphasize is the importance of developing one's theological imagination by learning to meditate upon certain texts in Scripture that, although generally avoided, seem designed for the very purpose. Take, for instance, the book of Revelation. For the typical evangelical Christian, Revelation would hardly be the place to practice meditation. Why let the Christian imagination loose on a text that is already seemingly way too imaginative? As Jewish rabbis of the past have taught about Ezekiel 1, there are just certain texts that might be considered off-limits to the untutored mind.

In his excellent book *Lit!*, however, pastor and author Tony Reinke argues the very opposite. "No book in the Bible demands more from our imagination than the book of Revelation,"[25] he asserts (obviously forgetting, at least in our opinion, Ezekiel's four great visions). As a result, the book was, at first, lost upon him. He could not "understand" it, so, assuming that the intellect is the only relevant part of his mind, he put that portion of God's Word aside. Reinke had to learn, as many of us do, that "the imagination is a God-given ability to receive truth and meaning," that he had for years failed at "cultivating [his] imagination," that this failure led to "an unintended neglect of the imaginative literature of Scripture," and that so much of Scripture, including John's Revelation, "invites us to see ultimate reality through our imaginations."[26]

With that grand invitation in mind, we propose that you combine the discipline of Christian meditation with the imaginative texts of Scripture. Specifically, using either the three-part model mentioned above or another with which you are familiar, meditate on any or all of the richly theological visions of Ezekiel. The core units are Ezekiel 1:4–28; 8:1–18; 37:1–14; and 47:1–12. If you want to branch out, meditate on Isaiah 6 or Revelation 4 and 5. You will find, as we have, that the Spirit of God delights to use these great texts in a distinctive way: to wash your soul from the grime of idolatry without and within, to draw your mind away from things visible, to God invisible, and thereby to expand your vision of the Lord God Almighty himself. And as such texts expand your theological imagination, you will undoubtedly be tasting the goodness of the Lord as Ezekiel did among the exiles by the Chebar Canal.

Lord, we praise you for yourself! Out of your infinity and your unlimited creative power, you deigned to create this universe in all of its order and complexity, beauty and wonder. And you deigned to create us. And as if that were not enough, you created us in your own image so that we too have personality and love, rationality and imagination. In our sin, we vandalized your image, and now we use those very powers you gave us against you and against our neighbors. But in your most awe-inspiring work of all, you sent your only Son—the image of the invisible God—into our flesh, redeeming us by his blood so as to restore your image in us. Help us to know you more completely through your written and incarnate Word. In his name we pray, Amen.

3

Imagination and Evil

So I lifted up my eyes toward the north and, behold, north of the altar gate, in the entrance, was this image of jealousy.

Ezekiel 8:5

We have kissed away kingdoms and provinces.

Scarus, a military officer, commenting on the effect
of Antony and Cleopatra's sinfully obsessive love
affair, in Shakespeare's *Antony and Cleopatra*

From Gene

We wanted to title our book simply *Imagine*. But that title was taken. John Lennon's signature song with that name, with its lovely melody and uplifting sentiments, asks us to imagine a world without God, without an afterlife, without religion. Above us is "only sky." And if we can imagine such a world, he sings—one that also lacks countries and possessions—we can further imagine "all the people" living in peace, unity, and happiness. We may say John is a dreamer—someone who lives in his imagination—but he is not the only one. The message of the song is that if we could all just imagine such a wonderful Godless world, that we could make it a reality.

The real imaginative achievement of this song—which *Rolling Stone* proclaimed the third "greatest song of all time"[1]—is that it manages to turn atheism, which is usually portrayed even by atheists as a bleak and depressing worldview, into a happy, utopian, flower-power paradise. Nietzsche stared into the abyss. John Lennon stares into the sunny blue sky. The pleasant melody and the pretty imagery take the edge off the song's message and make its nihilism seem pleasant and pretty too. The sad and plaintive quality of the melody, though, is a note of honesty that most people never notice. I have heard Christians earnestly sing "Imagine," apparently oblivious to the meaning of what they were singing.

To be able to write a song like that is, indeed, a sign of true artistic and imaginative talent. Moreover, the song makes a powerful point, whether intentionally or not. Atheism *is* an act of the imagination. Nihilism *is* an imaginative construction of the human mind. In fact, all false religions are made up by human beings using their creative imagination and then projecting their mental creations outward onto the world as doctrines, institutions, and customs. Such imaginatively made religions involve the creation of what the Bible calls "idols"—"images"—and the religious systems that grow around these images the Bible calls "idolatry."

The same can be said of false worldviews. We often assume that someone with a particular worldview has assembled it as a cerebral process, forming an individual philosophy based on rationally determined beliefs, whether correct or incorrect. This can certainly be a factor to some extent and with some people. But more often, a worldview begins as an imaginative construction, perhaps as an effort to build a model to account for empirical observations, isolated truths, and personal experiences. Many people, arguably, do not go to this trouble but rather let their worldview imaginations be influenced by other people's worldview imaginations. This explains why worldviews are often caught rather than taught. This applies also to the biblical worldview, which underscores the importance of cultivating a Christian imagination.

We can also sin in our imagination. This is one of the most important and yet neglected battlegrounds in the Christian life. Sins that we would never dare to commit we fantasize about doing, and Jesus is clear that what goes on in our heart condemns us before God.

So our imagination, tainted as it is by the fall, can lead us away from God and into a whole range of idolatries and sin. The solution is not to suppress the imagination—which cannot really be done—but to restore it so that it helps rather than hinders us in our Christian living. The Bible also tells us how our imagination can help us not only to fight sin (the negative side of moral action) but also to love our neighbors (the positive side of God's commands). The Bible also stands as a work of God's imagination, as it were, which can shape the imagination of those who read and hear it.

Imagination and Sin

The human imagination—like the understanding and the will—is fallen, to the point of being a fountain of sin. "God saw that the wickedness of man was great in the earth, and that every imagination of the thoughts of his heart was only evil continually" (Gen. 6:5 KJV). This provoked God's judgment in the flood, but even after that cataclysm, the malady remains. The words are repeated after Noah's sacrifice and in the context of God's promises of grace:

And the LORD smelled a sweet savour; and the LORD said in his heart, I will not again curse the ground any more for man's sake; for the imagination of man's heart is evil from his youth; neither will I again smite any more every thing living, as I have done. (Gen. 8:21 KJV)

This suggests that even those who enjoy God's mercy and forgiveness still have a heart plagued with an evil imagination.

When we think of sins, we often think in terms of external actions, but Jesus sees even those external sins as issuing from a sinful heart: "For out of the heart come evil thoughts, murder, adultery, sexual immorality, theft, false witness, slander" (Matt. 15:19). Before a person commits such evil actions, he or she has imagined them, thought about them, and chosen them. The sin begins inside the person, which then can bear fruit in the world outside the self.

But the Bible makes very clear that these inner impulses, these imaginations of the heart, are sinful and incur God's judgment *even when the person never acts on them*, even when they remain inner fantasies or private emotions that never bear fruit in sinful actions. This is what Jesus teaches in the Sermon on the Mount:

> You have heard that it was said to those of old, "You shall not murder; and whoever murders will be liable to judgment." But I say to you that everyone who is angry with his brother will be liable to judgment. . . . You have heard that it was said, "You shall not commit adultery." But I say to you that everyone who looks at a woman with lustful intent has already committed adultery with her in his heart. (Matt. 5:21–22, 27–28)

Murderous and adulterous thoughts deserve God's judgment, just as overt murder and adultery do.

In fact, God particularly loathes that kind of interior sinning, which is often masked by an external show of righteousness. Among the things that God absolutely "hates," according to Solomon, is a "heart that deviseth wicked imaginations" (Prov. 6:18 KJV).

Our problem is not just *sins*—the bad things we do—but *sin*, the twisted proclivity of our inner lives. We can sometimes discipline ourselves to stop overt sinful actions while keeping alive the inner sinfulness that gave rise to them. We thus call down upon ourselves the woes Jesus pronounces on the hypocrites:

> Woe to you, scribes and Pharisees, hypocrites! For you clean the outside of the cup and the plate, but inside they are full of greed and self-indulgence. You blind Pharisee! First clean the inside

of the cup and the plate, that the outside also may be clean. Woe to you, scribes and Pharisees, hypocrites! For you are like white-washed tombs, which outwardly appear beautiful, but within are full of dead people's bones and all uncleanness. So you also outwardly appear righteous to others, but within you are full of hypocrisy and lawlessness. (Matt. 23:25–28)

Does this mean that sinning in the heart is just as bad as sinning in real life, so that we might as well just do the things that we imagine? No! External sin can be much more destructive than internal sin, just as external righteousness is worth cultivating despite a person's internal unrighteousness. If you commit adultery in your heart, you are harming your soul, but if you commit adultery in real life, you are harming your spouse, destroying your marriage, and devastating your family. If you commit murder in your heart with your inner anger and poisonous attitudes, you are liable to God's judgment, but if you actually commit murder, you are also liable to the judgment of the state, which can put you in prison or give you a lethal injection.

The "first use of the law," to use Reformation terminology, is specifically to restrain external evil so as to make life in this sinful world possible. We sinners would tear each other apart and society would become impossible if it were not for the moral law, which makes us feel ashamed and embarrassed to commit certain actions, especially if someone could see us. We are also prevented from indulging in our sinful tendencies by God-given institutions such as lawful governments, the family, and other social entities, whose tenets we fear to transgress. Such external compliance is called "civil righteousness." It is extremely important.

But spiritually, civil righteousness—however necessary to a happy life in this world—does not equate to righteousness before God, "who knows the heart" (Acts 15:8). But we can hardly control what comes into our minds! How can we possibly overcome sin at this level?

If we are "liable to judgment" for what goes on in the deepest recesses of the heart, we have to be doomed!

Indeed, we have to cry out with the apostle Paul, as he confessed the inescapability of sin in his own life: "Wretched man that I am! Who will deliver me from this body of death?" (Rom. 7:24). But this cry of desperation is immediately followed by the answer: "Thanks be to God through Jesus Christ our Lord!" (Rom. 7:25). And then the astonishing revelation:

> There is therefore now no condemnation for those who are in Christ Jesus. For the law of the Spirit of life has set you free in Christ Jesus from the law of sin and death. For God has done what the law, weakened by the flesh, could not do. By sending his own Son in the likeness of sinful flesh and for sin, he condemned sin in the flesh, in order that the righteous requirement of the law might be fulfilled in us, who walk not according to the flesh but according to the Spirit. (Rom. 8:1–4)

There is no condemnation for those who are in Christ Jesus! We certainly are liable to judgment, but Jesus took not just our sins but our sin, our sinful flesh—which has to include our evil imaginations—into himself, taking into himself also the judgment they deserve, setting us free!

We dare not ever come before God in the pretension of our own righteousness, as if we did not need Jesus and his cross. Honestly owning up to our inner sin and its contradictions with even the best efforts of our external lives impels us to throw ourselves upon Jesus. The heart is the locus of sin, but it is also the locus of faith (Rom. 9:10). Sin dwells in the heart, but so does the Holy Spirit (Gal. 4:6). And this good news, this gospel, is *not* an imaginative construct but a revelation from God himself, something no one could have imagined:

> But, as it is written,

"What no eye has seen, nor ear heard,
　　nor the heart of man imagined,
　what God has prepared for those who love him"—

these things God has revealed to us through the Spirit. For the
Spirit searches everything, even the depths of God. (1 Cor. 2:9–10)

Imagination and Good Works

There is no condemnation for those who are in Christ, but they still
battle sin. And as they grow in their faith, they grow in their holiness,
their sanctification. The apostle Paul describes the Christian life in
terms of an inner conflict, variously described as between the flesh
and the Spirit (Romans 8; Galatians 5), or the old self and the new
self (Romans 6; Col. 3:9). Christians must still contend with the evil
imaginations of their heart. But they can do so with the Spirit-given
faith that is living and active in their heart.

Just as indwelling sin bears fruit in sinful actions, faith bears fruit
in good works (James 2:14–17). But the good works acceptable to
God go beyond the external compliance of civil righteousness. They
must be motivated from the heart. We must not only stop harming
our neighbors and do good to them. We must love them.

Jesus repeatedly tells us that we are to love God with our whole
being and to love our neighbors as ourselves (Matt. 22:37–40).
Doing this requires "faith working through love" (Gal. 5:6). Faith
enables us to love God, because we are now reconciled to him. Faith
also enables us to love our neighbors as ourselves, because we see our
neighbors in ourselves.

This requires a sanctified imagination. Consider the Golden Rule:
"So whatever you wish that others would do to you, do also to them,
for this is the Law and the Prophets" (Matt. 7:12). This is another way
of saying, "Love your neighbor as yourself." You love yourself, so love
your neighbor in the same way. You must imagine your neighbor as

someone like yourself. Imagine how you would like your neighbor to treat you, and then treat your neighbor in the same way.

Or consider the apostle Paul's injunction to "rejoice with those who rejoice, weep with those who weep" (Rom. 12:15). This is a call for *empathy*, the act of imaginatively putting yourself in the position of another person to the point of imaginatively feeling what that person feels.

Or consider the work of the imagination called for in other passages from Scripture on how we are to treat one another. "Bear one another's burdens, and so fulfill the law of Christ" (Gal. 6:2).[2] "If one member suffers, all suffer together; if one member is honored, all rejoice together" (1 Cor. 12:26).

Faith in the gospel of Christ is what enables this kind of empathetic love of the neighbor. For one thing, the true knowledge of one's own sinfulness—which is a prerequisite of faith—destroys our pride, that egotism that is the major obstacle in loving another person. According to Mary, the mother of our Lord, the gift of her Son is particularly devastating to a proud person's imagination: "He hath scattered the proud in the imagination of their hearts" (Luke 1:51 KJV). The other major obstacle to loving the neighbor is that person's sinfulness. We dislike people largely for the bad things they do. We judge them much more harshly than we judge ourselves. But by faith, I know the magnitude of my sin and the greater magnitude of Christ's forgiveness of my sin. This can only make me more forgiving of my neighbor's sin. If Christ forgave me, how can I not forgive my neighbor?[3] But doing this takes imagination.

In short, the imagination is the source of idolatry and also a means of contemplating truth. It is a source of sin, and it is a source of good works. This polarity is suggested in Scripture. The ancient Greeks were masters of the imagination, both in their intellectual, literary, and artistic greatness and in their idolatry. So when Paul addressed the Athenians in the Areopagus, he quoted one of their poets and showed the contradictions in their own theology: "Being then God's offspring, we ought not to think that the divine being is like gold or silver or stone, an image formed by the art and imagination of man" (Acts 17:29). The solution to the idolatrous, sinful imagination is a godly, righteous imagination. Thus King David, when he dedicates the temple—which itself addresses the imagination of God's people with its art, architecture, music, and rituals—recalls the history of human sin and of God's saving grace. He concludes with a prayer that God would keep these truths in his people's *imagination*: "O LORD God of Abraham, Isaac, and of Israel, our fathers, keep this forever in the imagination of the thoughts of the heart of thy people, and prepare their heart unto thee" (1 Chron. 29:18 KJV).

From Matt

Before the beginning, God imagined. In the beginning, he created. And sometime after the beginning, Adam and Eve sinned. And on the day of that first disobedience, God's warning came to pass: Adam and Eve "surely" died (Gen. 2:17).

That death was, first of all, spiritual. After all, Adam and Eve did not immediately fall to the earth in rigor mortis after eating the forbidden fruit. Physical death would come later. But they did immediately die in their spirits; fatally destructive forces of separation entered their hearts, cutting them off from each other, from the created world, and from God himself. Paradise was lost, as "sin came into the world . . . and death through sin" (Rom. 5:12).

The sin of our first parents bent the Tree of the Knowledge of Good and Evil toward evil. From that day forward, every similar "tree," every gift of God designed for our potential blessing, has been marred by the destructive forces of sin. Each such gift in itself is not what it would have been otherwise had Adam and Eve not sinned.

Alas, ours is now a fallen world. And, to make matters worse, the sinfully distorted gift can in turn be further distorted by the user and bent toward either of two goals: good or evil. So much depends on the users, on what we, the children of Adam and Eve, choose to do with the gift. In itself and in its using, God's creation has fallen into sin.

This doubly cursed reality of God's creation most certainly applies to the human imagination. On the one hand, imagination is capable of great blessing. Consider the early chapters of Genesis, where we read about Jabal and Jubal, sons of Adah, sons of Adam (Gen. 4:20–21). Their descendants created tents and developed the nomadic culture that went with them; they imagined the possibility of domesticating animals and did so; they invented harps and lyres and became creative masters of their music. These are remarkable advances of human civilization that bespeak the common-grace power of human imagination, even in its fallen condition.

On the other hand, the opening chapters of Genesis also describe instances of sinfully destructive imagination. Lamech, descendant of Adam through Cain and Enoch, twisted the imaginative capacity to devise a scrap of poetry, most likely a song, in which he celebrated his audacious chutzpah as a murderer (Gen. 4:23–24). Not to betray my musical preferences or cast aspersions on the radio tastes of some of my best friends, but might his lyric be the first bit of country music ever recorded? (Note from Gene, author of *Honky Tonk Gospel*: no!) Regardless, it is a low point in the primeval history of imagination. Equally low is the sinful hubris captured several chapters later when Adam's descendants, now dispersed as far east as the plains of Shinar, imagine that they can build a tower "with its top in the heavens" (Gen. 11:4). Their work, the Tower of Babel, could be considered one of the most pathetic works of human imagination ever devised in the history of evil and good, looking ahead to the evil visions of more recent tragedies: Hitler's Third Reich, the Khmer Rouge, or

Darfur genocide. All these and so much more are just the repeated rebellions of the fallen human imagination, which sets itself against the Lord and his Anointed, delusionally believing it can "burst their bonds apart and cast away their cords from us" (Ps. 2:3). No wonder the Genesis account tells us that the Lord "saw that the wickedness of man was great in the earth, and that every intention of the thoughts of his heart was only evil continually" (Gen. 6:5).

It should come as no surprise, therefore, that as God recaptures the exiled generation of Ezekiel by means of visions, he does not hesitate to fill the prophet's imagination with full reality, images of unspeakable evil. In chapter 8, Ezekiel is transported by the Spirit to Jerusalem,[4] where, in what seems to be some strange out-of-the-body experience, the prophet has paraded before him all sorts of idolatrous abominations taking place in the temple itself. Given some of the details in chapters 8 through 11, it is virtually certain that the scenes were not occurring simultaneous to one another or even in the real-time presence of the prophet. Instead, it is better to understand that the scenes Ezekiel beholds provide a perverse anthology of the types of abominations (a term that Ezekiel uses six times in chaps. 8 and 9) that had been going on. That is why ritual details, locations, and names are included. What the prophet beholds is, sadly, reality, although not necessarily reality at the very moment of his prophetic visitation.

You could think of Ezekiel's first Jerusalem trip as a supernatural documentary compiled by none other than the Lord himself. Gritty in its realism, designed to haunt the prophet with its images of evil, the documentary has an overwhelming effect. It inundates Ezekiel with the terrifying realization of how high and wide and deep is the idolatry of his contemporaries, so much so that at one point he cries out, "Ah, Lord GOD! Will you destroy all the remnant of Israel in the outpouring of your wrath on Jerusalem?" (Ezek. 9:8).

Ezekiel's second vision unavoidably confronts us too, presenting both directly and indirectly some of the dilemmas that surround our God-given but deeply fallen imagination in relation to human sin and evil. The Christian's imagination can be either a dangerous friend of evil or its weighty foe. So to help us think about the imagination in relation to evil, I want to make two strategic moves with the Ezekiel text. Given the length of the second vision (chaps. 8 through 11), I will make my moves in relation to the opening section of the vision, i.e., the set of scenes found in Ezekiel 8:1–18.

The Terrifying Whole of Idolatry

Ezekiel's second vision is launched during an elders' meeting. As a senior pastor for nearly thirty years, I have seen and heard just about everything you could imagine in the course of over five hundred elders' meetings, but nothing can match this one. It is a September day in Babylon, and while the prophet is seated facing "the elders of Judah"[5] who are in exile with him, the "hand of the Lord God" interrupts the session by falling upon the prophet in a forceful, almost violating, way. The normal is contravened, and in some sort of visionary trance, Ezekiel's imagination is briefly filled once more with the vision from the summer before (for us, the vision of chapter 1), a vision of the Lord God as both a man and the omnipresent King of providence, the Lord of simultaneous and infinite workings. This "fiery one" (see Ezek. 8:2), who has flames below his waist and glowing metal above, collaborates with the divine Spirit (or wind or breath). Together they pick Ezekiel up out of the room (through the ceiling?), on up and up as high as "between earth and heaven" (we might say, mid-atmosphere) and then transport the prophet to the holy city. With such a forceful opening to the second vision, our imagination is engaged, and rightly so, for what follows will demand of us even more.

The terrifying opening scene gives way to four scenes even more shocking. In rapid succession, the prophet is asked to gaze upon what were for him disgusting abominations, foul forms of idolatry that were anathema to anyone with a sensitive Torah-trained conscience, especially for someone who had been trained since youth to serve as a priest in the most holy temple of the one true God.

If you take a look at each of the four scenes, you observe a terrifying sequence. In the first one, Ezekiel sees an "image of jealousy" standing some distance from the temple gate, toward the north entrance to the city (Ezek. 8:5). Given its location on the north side of Jerusalem, the side from which enemies would have attacked, the pole must undoubtedly have served in some sort of protective role, guarding the people from assaults, replacing God himself as the city's protector. Based on the description, one can presume that this was some sort of Asherah pole or tall phallic symbol. The use of the word *jealousy* as a descriptor most likely points to the covenant offense that this was to the Lord himself, whose jealousy would rightly be triggered by such effrontery. In whom, after all, were his people trusting? The Lord had promised repeatedly that he would be the guardian of his beloved city. As one of the Jerusalem psalms states, "Within her citadels God has made himself known as a fortress" (Ps. 48:3). But trust in an invisible God had obviously worn thin, and a sanctified imagination was replaced by an idolatrous pole, conceived in the fantasies of the fleshly mind.

After looking toward the north of the city, Ezekiel travels (better, is carried) to the entrance of the temple courtyard (Ezek. 8:7). There, he is commanded to dig through a hole in the wall. Upon doing so, he stumbles into an inside room, where he beholds "seventy men of the elders of the house of Israel" waving incense offerings to "every form of creeping things and loathsome beasts," which were "engraved on the wall all around" (vv. 10–11). Clearly, then, the idolatry has defaced the gates of the city; it has invaded the outer storage rooms of the temple itself.

But still more and worse are to come. We are taken, with the prophet, to the north entrance to the temple court, which lay on a side of the temple away from its main entrance, a side with limited accessibility from the city. This area, while certainly more prominent than the storage rooms in the previous scene, was still somewhat concealed from the main traffic in and out of the holy complex. But there, too, idolatry is discovered, as the prophet openly sees yet another scene of abominable worship: in this case, women "weeping for Tammuz" (v. 14).[6] Tears are being shed, to be sure, but tears for the very wrong thing: tears for the idols, not tears because of the idols.

And still more and still worse are to come. For the final scene, Ezekiel is brought inside the temple courtyard, to the "inner court" (v. 16) that lay before the main entrance, between the temple steps and the altar of sacrifices. There the prophet beholds a couple dozen men who are caught, as before, in flagrante delicto, in the unfaithful act of worshiping the sun. Their faces are toward the east, which means, as Ezekiel assiduously notes, that the prostrate devotees have their back sides thrust out against the temple, a sign of contemptuous disregard for the Lord God and his holy mount.[7]

"Have you seen this?" the fiery one demands of Ezekiel at some point during each of the four scenes. It is a rhetorical question, forcing Ezekiel to see with his mind and imagination as well as with his eyes. And certainly what Ezekiel saw must have been totalizing in its power, for the abominations of idolatry progressed closer and closer to the very heart of the temple. The Most Holy Place was clearly in jeopardy of being desecrated. No wonder that later in this second vision, the glory of the Lord departs from the temple (10:4) and eventually even from Jerusalem (11:23). God in his judgment abandons his chosen city. The glory of God and the ugliness of idolatry are mutually exclusive.

I want to call your attention to another progression that runs through Ezekiel's vision and its four scenes. Like the first, this second progression points to the vision's totalizing power. If you were to list all the different types of people involved in these scenes of idolatry, and along with them all the different gods, you would make a sobering discovery. Taken in combination, all four scenes of abomination involve every sort of person and every sort of god. Men and women are worshiping false gods. Ordinary people are offering evil sacrifices alongside leaders and elders. Gods from the surrounding nations are being bowed down to: the sun god and Tammuz from Babylon, reptiles and creeping things from the abundance of Egyptian idolatries. No one seems to be excepted; no place seems to be immune. The idolatry of Ezekiel's contemporaries has fastened itself deeply into everyone, everywhere, in the holy city, and it is drawing upon all the false religions of nations on every side. Sadly, Jerusalem's idolatry knows no bounds; it is sinfully comprehensive.

The idolatry Ezekiel witnesses is also frightening in its effect over time. In short, it degenerates, undoing the spiritual life and wholeness that are to be found in covenant life with the Lord God. Note, for instance, the reference in 8:11 to one Jaazaniah, the son of Shaphan. He is singled out by name from among the larger group of those who were waving incense offerings before graven images inscribed upon the walls. His name is not an unnecessary detail inserted by the prophet as a move in some sort of now-lost personal vendetta. Rather, there is a history here, and a degenerative one. Jaazaniah's older relatives had provided godly leadership during King Josiah's religious and temple reforms some twenty-five years earlier. We know this because of the narrative in 2 Kings 22:8–10, which tells how Shaphan read the newly discovered Book of the Law to the king and later consulted with the prophetess (2 Kings 22:14–20). But now, how the mighty have fallen! The passing of a quarter century has made all the difference in a family's faith commitments. Jaazaniah has defiled the inspiring story of his father's bravery. Idolatry can erode even the strongest of heritages.

And there is more. A similar demonstration of idolatry's degenerative effects is captured in another of Ezekiel's seemingly off-hand comments. Again in 8:11, the prophet makes mention of seventy elders who, like Jaazaniah, are busy offering incense to images graven on the chamber walls. "Seventy elders": it is no coincidence that a different set of seventy elders is described in the book of Exodus. There, they are worshiping the true God, the Lord, on Mount Sinai during a covenant renewal with Moses (see Exodus 34). The contrast between the Exodus and Ezekiel scenes tells the same story as Jaazaniah's family tree: idolatry pollutes and perverts, invading even the strongest circles of commitment and degenerating God's people over time.

One final comment is worth making. The totalizing, comprehensive, and degenerative power of idolatry might have been more easily resisted by Ezekiel's Jerusalem contemporaries were it not for its blinding effect. There is a deep irony in the question of Ezekiel 8:12, asked of the prophet with respect to the same scene of seventy elders caught in idolatrous worship: "Son of man, have you seen what the elders of the house of Israel are doing in the dark?" Of course the prophet is able to see it; he writes about it vividly; his imagination can still see it as he records his prophecy. The question is deeply rhetorical. In fact, it plays like a repeated bass note throughout the entire passage. Four other times Ezekiel is asked by the fiery one who is escorting him, "Son of man, have you seen this?" (see vv. 6, 9, 15, 17). Have you seen this? Have you really seen this? Do you see it with the same eyes as I, the Lord? Certainly Ezekiel sees it. And we do too. But perhaps not as much as we should! The question is worth pondering. But what is unquestionably true is that Jaazaniah and the seventy elders and all the others in chapter 8 are like the gathered crowd in the final scene of the emperor's new clothes. None of them can really see what is starkly evident to any and all outsiders: idolatry blinds. The only people who cannot see it and its effects for what they are, are the idolaters themselves.

The point of these various exposés of idolatry is this: idolatry in Ezekiel's Jerusalem ran deep. It had all levels of society and types of people in its grasp. It degenerated even the best of them. And its coup de grace was that they could not recognize what had happened. Out of that matrix of ideas an important principle emerges. In relation to the role of imagination in the Christian life, idolatry stands out as a key concept. The main reason idolatry has such totalizing power is that, at bottom, idolatry is an act of the human imagination. It is an attempt to make visible what cannot be seen. If you temporarily put to the side the very real demonic component of idolatry,[8] what you have left is chiefly its imaginative side. Idolatry is an attempt of the imagination to take the divine and make it visible, to make it understandable, to make it manageable. It is one's imagination that gives life to what have been called "counterfeit gods": false realities that, if consented to by one's imagination, gain such existential, religious, and life force that they function as powerful (and empowering) deities.[9] The Lord himself talks to Ezekiel about the terrifying results when one allows idols to couple with one's imagination. The actual phrase is taking "his idols into his heart," and when this takes place, dire consequences await:

> Therefore speak to them and say to them, Thus says the Lord GOD: Any one of the house of Israel who takes his idols into his heart and sets the stumbling block of his iniquity before his face, and yet comes to the prophet, I the LORD will answer him as he comes with the multitude of his idols, that I may lay hold of the hearts of the house of Israel, who are all estranged from me through their idols. (Ezek. 14:4–5)

Estrangement. A stumbling block of iniquity. Anyone of the house of Israel—including religious elders and leaders. God clearly understands the power of imagination in the battle against evil.

Enemy and Ally

Imagination, when detached from God's truth, can be a malevolent ally of evil. You can see this in three different ways. First, when unleashed, imagination spawns idolatry. It is the imagination rather than cool reason that lies behind John Calvin's famous dictum that "the human heart is a veritable factory of idols." Why do I say that? Well, reason through it with me. We human beings discover something that seems to work on a limited basis (money, sex, power, knowledge, physical force, deceit) and then proceed to broaden it out. Our imagination joins with the "thing" and conceives a system of homage and devotion and behavior that goes with it. Imagination, not reason, is what generally spawns idolatry.

Second, our fallen imagination is what leads into temptation. Puritan author Thomas Brooks aptly describes the way Satan likes to bait the hook when we are tempted. The Evil One deftly wraps the sting of sin with some sort of tasty worm—a promise of what our lives can be like if we choose this course of action (a.k.a. sin), a picture of the happy selves we will be if we say yes, a lie that we will not surely die. I do not deny the great Tempter's role in doing this sort of thing,[10] but what I want to add is that he could get nowhere were it not for a consenting and promiscuous imagination. Chief among the spiritual enemies within our own flesh is our fallen imagination itself. As Jesus himself says, "Out of the heart [which, I am saying, includes as one of its principal parts the imagination] come evil thoughts[11] [products of our fertile mind, which again includes our fertile imagination]. . . . These are what defile a person" (Matt. 15:19). The connection between imagination and temptation is deep.

Finally, the fallen imagination prevents us from seeing what sin is doing to us. While it is true that sin eventually finds us out, imagination does an effective job of masking sin's effects, at least for a while. As we saw with Ezekiel, the persistent question is, "Do you see this?" and its answer too often is, "What?" Literature abounds with stories of such self-deception. Take, for instance, Gollum, the pitiful nemesis of Frodo in J. R. R. Tolkien's *The Lord of the Rings*. Formerly a hobbit, he has slowly fallen under the curse and power of the one ring, and apart from decreasingly frequent moments of inner turmoil in which his good self, Smeagol, argues with his fallen self, Gollum, he lives unaware of his captured self. An even more potent story is that told in Oscar Wilde's *The Picture of Dorian Gray*. In it, a dashing young blade, Dorian Gray, is urged on by his imaginative powers and falls into successively deeper temptations with seeming impunity. But, alas, his sin must find him out. A portrait of himself up in his attic becomes a little more perverse each time he chooses evil, and in the end the picture tears apart, and simultaneously Dorian's sin disfigures him in all its repulsiveness.

So, yes, imagination can be a malevolent ally of evil. But it can also be a powerful friend of the good. Think carefully about the appeals to a Christian imagination embedded in these various New Testament texts:

> Consider the lilies of the field, how they grow: they neither toil nor spin, yet I tell you, even Solomon in all his glory was not arrayed like one of these. (Matt. 6:28–29)

> For this light momentary affliction is preparing for us an eternal weight of glory beyond all comparison, as we look not to the things that are seen but to the things that are unseen. (2 Cor. 4:17–18)

> Let us run with endurance the race that is set before us, looking to Jesus, the founder and perfecter of our faith. (Heb. 12:1–2)

> Though you have not seen him [that is, Christ], you love him. Though you do not now see him, you believe in him and rejoice with joy that is inexpressible and filled with glory. (1 Pet. 1:8)

> I saw in the midst of the lampstands one like a son of man, clothed with a long robe and with a golden sash around his chest. The hairs of his head were white, like white wool, like snow. His eyes were like a flame of fire. (Rev. 1:13–14)

Do you see how all of these texts, each in its own way, underline the importance of imagination in the Christian life? Jesus tells his hearers to imagine the way lilies grow. Paul tells us to look with our imagination's eyes to the things that are unseen. Hebrews tells us to keep our imagination fixed on Jesus. Peter talks about loving someone you have not seen. Revelation describes in detail the glory of the resurrected Lord, inviting our imagination to assemble a living collage of our frighteningly awesome God. Each text in its own way challenges the Christian to turn his imagination to good, to intentionally direct the eye of his heart toward Christ as glorious Lord and his gospel as our all-controlling story. The imagination is indeed the eye of the soul, and our Lord had it at least partly in mind when he explained that "the eye is the lamp of the body. So, if your eye is healthy, your whole body will be full of light, but if your eye is bad, your whole body will be full of darkness. If then the light in you is darkness, how great is the darkness!" (Matt. 6:22–23).

To that end, then, let us consider an important privilege available to us, one we can apply to help turn imagination's eye away from evil and toward good—namely, confession.

Colloquy

When we confess, we agree with someone else and say with that person the same thing. For example, when we recite a statement of faith such as the Nicene Creed, saying, "We believe . . . ," we are saying with God the same thing about him as he says about himself, and we are saying it with the entire Christian church. Or again, when we give testimony to others that we are Christians, we make the good confession that Christ is our Lord and God; that is, we say with God and his gospel that Jesus Christ is, in our lives, who he claims to be. When we confess our sin, we are again saying the same with someone else. In this case, we are saying with God that the stated things we have done are wrong and sinful, that they have caused him grief and have relationally come between us.

There are two sides to the confession of sins. One side is ours, and the other side is God's. When we confess our sins to God (our side), God confesses back to us by his Word and through his Spirit that we are forgiven, that we are washed clean and justified freely through Christ's death and resurrection (his side). Our sin and its old self inside us are taken off; Christ's imputed righteousness is rediscovered, and his resurrection life is joyfully put on afresh.

Because of the tendency in our day and age to shrink imagination to the creative impulse, there is a tendency to give imagination a free ride when it comes to sin and confession. "We don't need to go there," one says. "After all, imagination arises spontaneously. That's why the Greeks and Romans used to think of it as a 'divine attendant spirit that came to human beings from some distant and unknowable source.'"[12] Such a view of our imagination amounts to nothing more than outsourcing it, and while there is a measure of truth to imagination's seeming spontaneity, our imagination is still ours: we have to own it, assess it, and by God's grace transform it. Jesus gives us a good balance here. On the one hand, when referring to the lascivious imagination, Jesus talks about looking "at a woman with lustful intent" (Matt. 5:28). His careful wording distinguishes between impulse and intention, between imagination that is beyond our conscious control (the initial imagination that might arise in one's mind upon seeing someone with sexual appeal) and imagination that is chosen and deliberately enflamed (the "lustful intent" behind a second and prurient gaze). On the other hand, however, Jesus does speak about the defiling and corrupting impact of imagination, regardless of its intentionality. In Matthew 15:19 Jesus identifies those things that "defile a person," and first among them are "evil thoughts," a term we have already discussed as including chiefly the work of our imagination.

To put all this in the phraseology of the apostle Paul, both the old Adamic self and the new self in Christ prevail upon one's imagination. There is a set of fallen and corrupt imaginations inside the Christian, and there is a set of resurrected, God-honoring, life-giving imaginations. The first we must learn to identify, confess, and turn away from; the second we must identify, develop, and enjoy.

Think of it (imagine it) this way. Inside the heart of a Christian are two different design and production teams. Both teams have as their goal the creation and distribution of a set of streaming images and accompanying sound track, a movie. The first team is like Pixar. It has learned over time to turn out wholesome and uplifting films like *Toy Story, Finding Nemo,* and *WALL-E.* The second team, however, is darker. Like some B-level movie studio kicking out violence, flesh, and wickedness, this team has learned over time, in fact from the earliest days of your life, to produce disturbing movies full of seductive scenes, appalling violence, and relationship-destroying images. Think movies like *The Texas Chain-Saw Massacre* or *I Spit on Your Grave.*

Because of Christ's death and resurrection, you have both the opportunity and the responsibility to pull the funding from the B-level studio and redirect it to Pixar. In Christ you are called to take off the old and put on the new. And the first step, the strategic step, in doing so is to identify and confess daily before God the "design and production" efforts of the old self's imagination.

One tool that can help you to do this is the regular practice of an "imagination audit." Here are some simple steps or guidelines, if you will. They will not only help you learn how to do such an audit but also heighten your awareness of the role your imagination plays in glorifying God or pursuing evil.

1) For a whole week, three times a day, first thing in the morning, sometime around noon, and then again before going to bed, ask

yourself the following questions. You might want to jot down your answers for future reflection:

- What memories, dreams, or mental pictures have been particularly vivid? How have they been impacting me? How have they made me feel?

- Which of those mental pictures have been encouraging and life-giving? Which ones have been destructive and life-sucking?

- How do these mental pictures stack up against God's Word? (Be specific and place them alongside key texts such as the Ten Commandments or the Beatitudes or 1 Corinthians 13 or Colossians 3:1–17.)

- Is there an "imagination feed" behind these pictures, in other words, a network of visual or mental input, behaviors, relationships, and unopposed ruminating thoughts that as best I can tell give rise to these images?

- How would I characterize that imagination feed? How would the Lord assess it?

2) As you progress through the week, notice patterns, similarities, cycles, and time-of-day propensities. Again, jot them down for future comparison and reflection.

We suggest that as you grow in self-awareness through the audit, you begin to develop a plan for putting off the old imagination and putting on the new. Ezekiel's third vision, as developed in the next chapter, will help especially with the latter.

For now, be aware of the imaginings of your heart. Practice fighting back against those that are evil. Drive them back—as opposed to lingering on them, as we usually do—with those that are good. And try this: pray about them.

John Kleinig, in his brilliant book on Christian spirituality, *Grace upon Grace*, has a suggestion for when the mind wanders during times of prayer that should also serve well in the disciplining of the imagination. When we pray, our concentration often falters so that instead of concentrating on God, thoughts pop into our mind about what we are going to have for dinner, or a problem at work, or a resentment we have against a friend, or an anticipation of the weekend. When such distractions occur, Pastor Kleinig recommends using them as things to pray about! Thank God for that dinner you are anticipating; ask his guidance about that problem at work; pray for reconciliation with that friend; ask his blessing on the weekend. In doing so, you are bringing those distractions into the prayer. And since these are obviously things, as we say, "on our mind"—or "on our imagination"—they are honest concerns and preoccupations that we need to pray about.[13]

Try letting your mind wander, attending to what your imagination is conjuring up. Daydreaming about your upcoming family vacation? Pray for your family and your time together. A sinful sexual fantasy? Pray against that sin, asking God's forgiveness and for a pure heart. A disastrous scenario that might happen at work? Pray that God will keep that from happening and give you peace about it. A painful memory that you cannot get out of your head? Pray that God will heal you of that trauma. A fantasy about relaxing on the beach? Thank God for providing such a beautiful world and so many innocent pleasures. Such an exercise can become a habit, as you bring your imaginings to God and bring God to your imaginings.

> *Lord, we confess that we sin in our imaginations. Forgive us for our sinful fantasies and evil daydreams. Forgive us for the way we linger on them and treasure them, taking pleasure in wickedness that we would never dare to commit but that we indulge within our hearts. Cleanse us in the innermost reaches of our hearts and minds with the blood of your Son. Fill us in-*

stead with imaginings that lead us to empathy and compassion for our neighbors and praise for you. Cast down the idolatrous graven images that we construct from our imagination and replace them with the truth of your Word. Through Jesus Christ we pray, Amen.

Imagination and the Future

Son of man, can these bones live?

Ezekiel 37:3

The human being is the only animal
that thinks about the future.

Daniel Gilbert, research psychologist, Harvard University

From Gene

The imagination allows us to fix concrete reality into our minds. But it can do more. The imagination can be receptive (allowing us to contemplate what already exists), and it can also be creative (allowing us to formulate images of what does not exist or does not yet exist). One power of the imagination is memory, the ability to recall what happened in the past. The imagination can also look forward into the future, to make projections in the realm of potential, of what may or may not happen.

This creative faculty of the imagination makes possible the arts and every kind of invention. It makes possible the ordinary but quite necessary process of planning as well as the free-floating reverie we call "daydreaming." Being able to imagine the future—as well as the steps it will take to get there—is critical for self-discipline, prudence, and wisdom. Spiritually, when we contemplate imaginatively what we know by faith will happen—that God's promises will come to fruition, that Christ will never forsake us despite our troubles, that we will enjoy eternal life and, as Ezekiel sees, the resurrection of the dead—we exercise the spiritual virtue of hope.

The Primary and the Secondary Imagination

The great theorist of the imagination is Samuel Taylor Coleridge. You may know him as the renowned Romantic poet, the author of "Kubla Khan" and "The Rhyme of the Ancient Mariner." You may know him as the opium addict, whose drug compulsion stimulated his imagination to the point of hallucination and near madness. But his drug addiction—his inability to just choose to stop taking laudanum, despite the way it was ruining his life—led him to the study of Reformation theology and a profound apprehension of the gospel.[1] Despite and in some sense because of his struggles, Coleridge made pivotal contributions to the fields of literary criticism, psychology, political theory, philosophy, and theology, and he is recognized as one of the greatest minds of the nineteenth century.

In his *Biographia Literaria*, or "literary biography," in which he reflects on the literary revolution that he engineered with the help of his friend William Wordsworth, Coleridge distinguishes between two kinds of imagination. His explanation is rather dense, to say the least, but it is worth unpacking.

> The IMAGINATION then, I consider either as primary, or secondary. The primary IMAGINATION I hold to be the living Power and prime Agent of all human Perception, and as a repetition in the finite mind of the eternal act of creation in the infinite I AM. The secondary Imagination I consider as an echo of the former, co-existing with the conscious will, yet still as identical with the primary in the kind of its agency, and dif-

fering only in degree, and in the mode of operation. It dissolves, diffuses, dissipates, in order to recreate; or where this process is rendered impossible, yet still at all events it struggles to idealise and unify.[2]

For Coleridge, the primary imagination is the mind's faculty for apprehending and comprehending what we perceive with our senses. It resides at the deepest level of the human mind and is an important facet of our personal identity. Significantly, Coleridge goes so far as to connect the primary imagination with the very image of God: "a repetition in the finite mind of the eternal act of creation in the infinite I AM."

The primary imagination functions of itself, without any conscious effort at all, in the normal course of our lives, as we take in the world through our senses. The secondary imagination, though, is imagination that is activated and focused by the *conscious will*. What a power that is! For instance, "I will now think about what I am going to do next weekend." Or, "I will now try to figure out how to put together the bookshelf that has been sitting in its box for the past three weeks." Or, "I will now make up a story and decide what will happen to the main character." As you can see, the secondary imagination harnesses the immense powers of the underlying primary imagination and puts them under our control.

In the *Biographia Literaria* Coleridge is most concerned with the secondary imagination, which becomes the key faculty for literary creation. (This works, as he says, by *dissolving* things that already exist, by *idealizing* them and working them into a *unity*, and, above all, by *recreating* the creation.) What Coleridge calls the "secondary imagination" is essentially what we are calling the "creative imagination." But more needs to be said about the primary imagination and its connection to an important concept in contemporary evangelical thought, namely, worldview.

Immanuel Kant, Imagination, and Worldview

In the surveys of Western thought and culture that Christians often engage in, the Enlightenment is summarized as the Age of Reason, which is then followed by Romanticism, the Age of Emotion. Thus Christians often dismiss the Romantic poets and philosophers as mere subjectivists. That is part of the story, but, like tourists trying to see all of Europe from a bus in a week, we often go too quickly, passing by points of interest and learning about them only super-ficially. (By the way, the term *Romanticism* refers not to "love" but to the medieval genre of the romance, the tales of knights and their adventures—and, yes, their loves—which early nineteenth-century writers emulated in developing the fantasy genre and in restoring a pre-Enlightenment view of the world.)

When the so-called Romantics reacted against the Enlighten-ment, they did not do so simply by offering up strong emotions as an alternative to the Age of Reason. Rather, they submitted the Enlight-enment-era rationalism to a withering and highly rational critique. The key thinker in this project was the German philosopher Im-manuel Kant. Like other great philosophers, Kant made extremely important contributions, while also opening up new vistas for wrong ideas. His understanding of the creative power of the human mind looms behind Coleridge's work on the imagination. And while Kant opened the door for postmodernism, with its skepticism and relativ-ism, he also laid the foundation for the worldview analysis practiced by contemporary evangelicals.

Though the Enlightenment claimed to be the Age of Reason, by reason they did not mean the use of logical syllogisms and deductive analysis (Christian thinkers such as Thomas Aquinas were the mas-ters of that approach, to a fault); rather, they emphasized inductive reasoning based upon empirical observation, as in the experimenta-tion of the new science. Enlightenment thinkers assumed that the mind is a blank slate, which receives sensory data and thus knowledge from the outside world.

Kant, however, showed that the human mind plays an active role in *shaping* that external data. For example, naïve empiricists might insist that they believe only what they see with their own eyes. In that case, though, they would have to believe that objects grow smaller as they move farther away. When they stand on a railway track, they would have to conclude that parallel lines meet, since the two sets of rails seem to grow closer together until they meet on the horizon. But they don't, despite what we see. Clearly, the mind has to interpret the data it perceives so that we can, as we say, "make sense of it."

The active power of the mind goes beyond the way we immediately process our sense perceptions according to the laws of perspective. We understand other kinds of knowledge by means of language, with its rules of grammar and classifications of concepts. Our minds sort what we experience and shape what we learn by means of categories, judgments, and other beliefs. We create mental models to filter out irrelevancies and to tie different kinds of information together.

This applies even to scientific knowledge. Much later, the pioneering historian of science Thomas Kuhn showed that the work of science is the creation of models to account for the data. When data is discovered that does not fit the prevailing model—after a period of resistance—a new model is created, resulting in a scientific "revolution."[3] Thus, the Ptolemaic model of the universe, with the earth at the center, explained and mathematically accounted for the observations of the stars and the planets—until new instruments such as the telescope found new data that led to the Copernican model, with the sun at the center. In physics, Newton's models gave way to Einstein's and then to those of the quantum physicists. Scientists first imagined atoms as hard little particles, then as minute solar systems, then as energy waves, and now—with quantum physics—they defy imagination all together, at least so far. In biology, Humboldt's assumption of the stable orderliness of nature gave way to Darwin's theory of evolution. Today, the Darwinian model is used to unify a whole range of scientific disciplines. We might ask scientists if they think Darwinism will still be the ruling paradigm five hundred years from now, or if new scientific paradigms will emerge as they always have. It may be that observations of the Intelligent Design theorists may be the bits of data that just aren't fitting with the current model, and that the fierce hostility the ID folks are experiencing—which is common in all scientific revolutions—may be a precursor to a new biological model in the future.[4]

Coleridge identified this active faculty of the mind, this model-making capacity, with the primary imagination, "the living Power and prime Agent of all human perception."[5] His friend William Wordsworth, who also became a conservative Christian, wrote one of his greatest poems about a beautiful landscape in Wales and how his memories of it and the meaning it had for him stay with him throughout his life. He refers to "all the mighty world / Of eye and ear,—both what they half create, / And what perceive."[6] One effect of Kant's thought was to make people skeptical about our ability to know objective truth and thus to cut off human beings from the external world beyond themselves. But, according to Alison Milbank, Coleridge and Wordsworth went beyond Kant to find a way to affirm "nature" as God's creation apart from the self.[7] They did so by considering the creation as the work of God's imagination, to which the human imagination must be aligned. Thus, for Coleridge, the primary imagination is not only "the Prime agent of all human perception," it is also "a repetition in the finite mind of the eternal act of creation in the infinite I AM."

While I hope you see the validity in some of what Kant says, I also hope you see the problems with his analysis and its consequences. Today's postmodernism grows out of Kantian philosophy. It's a small step to go from what the human faculties half create to what they totally create. If reality and knowledge are merely mental or imaginative "constructions," then truth is relative, and we must be skeptical about everything. Kant certainly did not go that far; rather, he remained an empiricist in insisting on the mind's dependence on its reception of external data. But he did drive a wedge between the objective universe—which became essentially unknowable in itself—and the subjective realm, from which we supposedly cannot escape. Kant's thought easily led to the exaltation of the self that we see especially in the lesser Romantic poets and artists, and it would lead inexorably to the "constructions" and "deconstructions" of contemporary postmodernism, whose critique of modernism is simply an echo of the Romantics' critique of the Enlightenment. At its worst, the notion that a human being "creates" his or her world usurps the true Creator and his works, putting man into the place of God, resulting in the rankest idolatry.

But Kant had another legacy. One of the many highly technical terms that Kant coined was *Weltanschauung*, that is, "worldview." His point was that we shape our perceptions, among other ways, according to our view of the world. But it took Calvinist thinkers such as James Orr, Abraham Kuyper, and the brilliant philosopher Herman Dooyeweerd, a critic of Kant who also built on his insights, to develop the concept of worldview and to put it into the service of Christian analysis.

"Conceiving of Christianity as a worldview," observed David Naugle, "has been one of the most significant developments in the recent history of the church."[8] Christianity is not only a set of doctrines, beliefs, and practices; it is also a way of looking at all of life and all the world. The Christian assumptions about human beings, nature, morality, God as the ultimate reality, what our problem is (sin), and how it is overcome (salvation through Christ), etc., all constitute a frame of reference, a worldview, in terms of which Christians think, perceive, and live.

But not only is Christianity a worldview; so are all other systems of belief. In his *Universe Next Door: A Basic Worldview Catalog*, James Sire examines deism, naturalism, nihilism, existentialism, Eastern monism, Islamic theism, and postmodernism as distinct worldviews with specific assumptions about human beings, nature, morality, ultimate reality, etc.[9] Dooyeweerd made the point that all such worldviews are essentially religious, including those that reject God as the ultimate reality. Our worldview becomes the paradigm through which we interpret everything. It is related to Kant's shaping intellect, to Coleridge's primary imagination.

Worldviews are often treated as a set of philosophical assumptions, which they are, but they are seldom arrived at by some rational intellectual exercise. Uneducated and nonreflective people have worldviews, no less than sophisticated philosophers (and the two groups often have the same beliefs). People's worldviews are shaped by their culture, the social groups they aspire to join, their experiences, and their desires. They are mental models, creatively assembled to make sense of life. Thus worldviews have to do with the imagination.[10] Worldviews are generally communicated and transmitted by works of the imagination—stories, music, art, drama, architecture, rituals, conversations, and cultural artifacts of every kind.

Postmodernists, like Christians, have adopted the concept of worldviews, which they conceive of as "interpretive paradigms," cultural or personal constructs, no one of which has any more validity than any other. Worldview thinking can indeed fall into relativism. In contrast, Christians believe that people tend to get entangled in false worldviews, that they need the true worldview that emerges from Scripture. Contrary to the Kantian extremists, objective truth is accessible, and Christians tend to agree with the classical thinkers that evidence, reason, and experience can lead us to truth about the world, though the truth of the Christian faith depends upon God's revelation, which he gives in his Word.

But imagination cannot be sidestepped. It is operative whether we want it to be or not. False worldviews—which are indeed imaginative constructs—can distort our faith. To cultivate a true worldview also requires exercising our imagination so that it accords with God's imagination—that is, his creation, his purposes, and his works of grace, all of which he reveals in his Word. Cultivating a Christian imagination is essential in cultivating a Christian worldview.

From Matt

Like millions of others, I was taken when the late Steven Jobs introduced Apple's iPad back in winter 2010. It was a gloomy moment in US culture. The country's Great Recession was mired in what would later be recognized as its lowest point, and the effects cast a dismal pall over the population—me included. Everything seemed so bleak and stationary: no movement, little confidence, even less optimism. And yet, in one of his signature product launches, Jobs cast a spell, even if fleeting, when he spoke of the iPad as "a magical and revolutionary device." The words took. In a follow-up communication, Jobs shared how a young man had written him about the magic of the iPad: "I was sitting in a café with my iPad," he wrote, and as a result of the device, a certain young woman paid a lot more attention to him. "Now that's what I call a magical device," he wryly e-mailed Jobs.

For me, happily married as I am, the iPad was magical in a much different way. My imagination was captured by its sleek design, its technological wizardry, its carefully thought-through interfaces, and its countless apps for countless situations. It seemed to combine simplicity and power in a wafer-thin device that, alas, was way beyond my budget. I could only dream.

And dream I did, like the millions of others who, like me, saw but did not buy. For several years I dreamed, until eventually, nearly three years later, I was able to purchase the dream: an iPad with the so-called retina display. And as I have come to find out, it is indeed sleek and powerful, and daily I do benefit from its technological servanthood. But all the dreams I dreamed under Jobs' promotional charm have not come true. My imagination had run way beyond reality. And contrary to American pop wisdom, simply because I imagined something did not bring it about.

Advertising tells us otherwise, however. It addresses our imagination and promises that a desirable future will be ours if we will only stop and buy. And if we do, our lives will be changed, the world will be different, human relationships will be transformed. Through pictures and stories and evocative scenes, advertising goes after the imagination. If you ever doubt the power of imagination, then just remember how much money goes into ads for the Super Bowl. As of 2013, a thirty-second spot went for as much as four million dollars. Mind you, these ads are purchased by successful corporations that know how to do business and spend money strategically. Obviously they have concluded that it is millions well spent to secure a spot during the Super Bowl. And that is because advertising is sheer imagination, and imagination is powerful. A well-constructed ad invites you to pay attention to a product you do not own and dream of what it would be like to possess it; all sorts of magical changes can result.

Advertising plays off imagination, and imagination plays off the future. So imagine for a moment what it would be like if the one being in the universe who does know the future, who in fact controls it, were to capture our imagination with striking promises about the future—promises that are entirely unlike Steven Jobs–like promotionals, which may or may not prove true. Rather, they are real promises of a definite future, promises of something you can count on happening.

It is therefore of no surprise that God, who first captured Ezekiel's imagination with a vision of his own glory (Ezekiel 1) and then followed with a sordid vision of depraved worship in Judah (chaps. 8–11), presents to the prophet yet another vision. This time, the vision is one of divine power so far-reaching that it interrupts the normative present, overturns it, and inaugurates an unanticipated future.

The Valley of Dry Bones

The vision is found in the first half of chapter 37, the "valley of the dry bones," as it is often called. It is only fourteen verses long, which makes this vision the shortest of Ezekiel's four. Despite its brevity, however, it is staggering. Pardon my foray into musical comparisons, but since Gene has already mentioned John Lennon and his song "Imagine," allow me a moment of liberty in relation to sixties music. One could liken Ezekiel's first vision to the Beatles first album, *Meet the Beatles*, a blitzkrieg musical invasion of the US by four creatures (John, Paul, George, and Ringo) from a distant land to the north. Following on, you could similarly compare the second vision to *The White Album*, a sprawling and often earthy exposure of the underbelly of the Fab Four. And with that said, the third vision is like *Revolver*: tightly constructed, unforgettable, mind-changing—the Beatles at their best.

The vision of dry bones is Ezekiel at his best, or at least at his most memorable. Some know of it through the familiar bit of folk doggerel often sung as a camp song: "The ankle bone's connected to the shin bone, and the shin bone's connected to the knee bone, and the knee bone's connected to the thigh bone: now hear the Word of the Lord." Others who hail from a liturgical background may know the vision through an Easter service, particularly if they are hardcore. In some Orthodox churches, the passage is read on Easter morning—well, more precisely, well after Saturday midnight during the wee hours; hence my reference to hardcore.

Ezekiel's third vision is intended to bring great hope to the captives in Babylon. It does so out of a seemingly unhopeful amalgam of elements. Among them are a trained priest, innumerable piles of bones, absurd words, and rushing wind. Let me first take a brief look at each of these elements. Then, combining them, I will draw two important connections: the first, between the vision and the exiles; the second, between the vision and us.

A Trained Priest

Before his deportation to Babylon in 597 BC at around age twenty-five, Ezekiel was preparing to serve as a priest in the Jerusalem temple. I say that because his father, Buzi, is identified as a priest in the opening verse of the book, and in light of the Torah pattern of priestly appointment through Levitical descent, Ezekiel was assuredly in training. It is an interesting exercise to imagine Ezekiel shadowing his father during the priestly course, learning firsthand about the ins and outs of slaughtering animal sacrifices—not a particularly pleasant set of images. There would also have been instruction in the prayers, benedictions, and festivals. Not only this, but the young Ezekiel would have taken to heart the priestly regulations concerning cleanliness and purity. So with all this in mind, imagine now the horror that Ezekiel would have had toward the essence of this vision, unburied human bones. It could very well have been the same sort of horror that is reflected in the covenant curses of Deuteronomy 28, which, through his training, would have been part of the priest-now-prophet's sensibilities: "The LORD will cause you to be defeated before your enemies. . . . And you shall be a horror to all the kingdoms of the earth. And your dead body shall be food for all birds of the air and for the beasts of the earth, and there shall be no one to frighten them away" (vv. 25–26).

The point is, let us not be glib or casual when we read about this vision and its valley filled with unburied human bones. For Ezekiel this was abomination! Revulsion! Certainly a valley to be avoided. The loathing Ezekiel must have felt could be compared to the New Testament scene in which Peter, *in a similarly revolting vision*, is commanded to eat all sorts of unclean animals. "By no means, Lord; for I have never eaten anything that is common or unclean," he replied (Acts 10:14). Peter was proud of his track record and resolved not to touch anything so disgusting as what was before him. Likewise, when Ezekiel was asked by the Lord to walk in among the unburied bones of his vision, his reaction could very well have been Petrine: "By no means, Lord; for I have learned well not to touch the unclean thing."

Innumerable Piles of Bones

We are told at the start of the vision that Ezekiel is "set . . . down in the middle of the valley" full of bones (Ezek. 37:1). It was the hand of the Lord that took him there, and no sooner is he placed in its midst than the same hand of the Lord leads him "around among them" (v. 2). "Around among": an interesting phrase with its doubled directions. Different translations handle it in different ways. The New Living Translation reads, "he led me all around among the bones"; the New International Version has, "he led me back and forth among them," while the King James Version has, he "caused me to pass by them round about." It is clear that the translations are struggling with the original, and from my way of thinking, part of the difficulty has to do with a default way of imagining the scene. If we think of the bones as strewn across the valley indiscriminately, then phrases such as "round about" make no sense. If, however, we picture the bones as piled into distinct heaps, one pile per soon-to-be-resurrected body, then the doubled prepositions make perfect sense. Guided by the hand of the Lord, Ezekiel picked his way between innumerable piles of bones, circling around each with extreme priestly caution so as to avoid any defiling contact. As he did so, he became only too familiar with the fact that each pile represented the remains of a single individual, an individual who, unknown to the prophet, would in a few short moments be rebuilt from toe to skull, wrapped in flesh, and then restored to life by the breath of the Creator.

Absurd Words

Sandwiched between the many piles of bones and an "exceedingly great army" of resurrected humans lay a conversation involving the Lord and his prophet. At two different points in this conversation, the Lord's words drew out the heart of Ezekiel. The conversation began with a question: "Son of man, can these bones live?" (v. 3). Ezekiel's answer is an easy-to-miss moment of great faith. He replies with extraordinary deference to divine mystery and power, saying "O Lord GOD, you know." In other words, that is your business, Lord. I do not want to deny your ability to do something that seems impossible to me, nor do I want to presume upon your intentions.

In terms of parallels, Ezekiel's submission here comes close to that of Mary, Jesus's mother, who, in response to Gabriel's revelation that the Messiah will be conceived within her as a result of the divine Spirit's power, replies, "Behold, I am the servant of the Lord; let it be to me according to your word" (Luke 1:38). Surrender. Submission. Deference to divine power in the face of human impossibility.

But there is more to Ezekiel's exchange with the Lord God. After the question and answer come divine command and human obedience. God tells Ezekiel to prophesy over the bones—to speak words into the air so as to deliver a divine promise ("I will cause breath to enter you, and you shall live," Ezek. 37:5) to mindless, soul-less, piles of dried human remains. These were absurd words to speak, absurd not just for the modern mind with its scientific categories of life and death but equally absurd for a sixth-century BC priestly mind with its years of experience in matters of life and death, bones and flesh, living sacrifices that, once slaughtered, are dead forever. And yet, in a much-overlooked moment of trusting obedience to divine command, Ezekiel prophesies to the bones, and the impossible happens. As he put it, "So I prophesied as I was commanded. And as I prophesied, there was a sound, and behold [that is, "Reader, stop! Think about this! Do so from my perspective! Be filled with amazement as was I!"], a rattling, and the bones came together, bone to its bone" (v. 7). [11]

What I find especially amazing about this moment in Ezekiel's ministry is his lack of pushback. So often in the accounts of Old Testament heroes, we read story after story of argument with God. "Are you sure, Lord? Don't you realize the obstacles to what you are asking?" But there was no argument from Ezekiel. For whatever reason, his faith, as reluctant or weak as it might have been, rose to the occasion.

A Rushing Wind

The unseen actor in this valley vision is the Spirit of God, and in the Hebrew he is all over the text. The word *ruah* occurs ten times in the twelve verses, translating as either Spirit, wind, or breath (see vv. 1, 5, 6, 8, 9 [four times],[12] 10, 14). The richness of this word, which is used in the text in many different senses, does a number of things. Chief among them is the way it locks this text into the account of creation in Genesis 2. There, God breathes (the verb used is the cognate for *ruah*) his life into a lifeless body made from dust, and as a result Adam becomes a living being. Here in Ezekiel, God breathes (the same verb as in Gen. 2:7) his breath (*ruah*) into lifeless bones, and as a result a whole valley of the dead becomes a host of living beings. Ezekiel's vision is an explicit reenactment of the first creation, but here it is speaking to a different type of creation, and to that we now turn.

Ezekiel's Dry Bones and the Crisis of the Exiles

As I have already discussed, the existential crisis of the Babylonian exiles was both extreme and real. And it is this third vision of Ezekiel's that most explicitly captures their state of heart. Ezekiel 37:11 is one of a dozen or so texts in the book that capture the profound angst and doubt of the exiles in Babylon. This text is especially poignant. Perhaps the best way for us to imagine the devastating loss—or the experience of it—that the Jews were feeling is to make an impossible comparison. As we did earlier, suppose again for just a moment, that an ancient coffin was unearthed in Jerusalem, and it was shown to contain, beyond any shadow of a doubt, the bones of Jesus of Nazareth. Jesus, in other words, had not been resurrected (at least in this contrary-to-fact illustration). Imagine, then, the bottom-fell-out disorientation and collapse of faith that would ensue for millions of Christians. "How can this be? We have staked our lives on an empty fiction? What do we do now?" It is these same sorts of questions that were filling the hearts of the Babylonian exiles. And in verse 11 they raise a collective three-part lament. Consider each of the parts in reverse order.

"We are indeed cut off," they cry. The strong verb "cut off" is unmistakably covenantal. We are unlinked from the promises made by Yahweh. We are rejected. The covenant is over. Yahweh has abandoned us. The connection between us and his promises is no more. We have been rejected. We are a God-forsaken people.

"Hope is lost." Unlike the modern use of the noun *hope*, the Old Testament's strong preference is for hope in its objective sense, i.e., the things we actually hope in as opposed to the confidence we have in them. The exiles are crying, "Any future that we might have had is now long gone. Our longed-for rescue has been dissolved." This second lament gives voice to the exiles' objectively dark reality, a world without God and without hope, which was a twisted version of their former creed.

"Our bones are dried up." I save this one for last because, of the three cries, it expresses most distinctively the interior reality of the exiles' experience. In the Old Testament, "bones" is an often unnoticed figure of speech. It is used in poetic and prophetic contexts to refer to one's emotions—more specifically, to one's underlying emotions, that is, one's drive, one's passion, one's vitalized soul. "Bones" is rather like our expression "gut," which is used to speak of our underlying feelings, our intuitions, our affections and disposition. "Our bones are dried up," the exiles say, and so they bewail the loss of their individual and collective soul, a soul that had been marked by profound trust in and love for the Redeemer.

To this grievous three-part lament the Lord God chose to answer with a prophet's unforgettable vision, not a verbal oracle. In other words, as has been the contention throughout this book, the creator God went after the exiles' imagination, their heart—their bones, to use the Old Testament figure. So, in its first and primary sense, the valley of dry bones vision must be read as an extended picture of what God can and will do with the "bones" of his people—their individual and collective hearts. In answer to each of the three laments, God makes specific promises.

1) To assure his people that he has not forgotten the covenant and that the exiles are not "cut off," God promises them that he will bring them back into the land that is theirs by covenant promise (vv. 12, 14).

2) To reseat his people in an objective hope, secured and established by the authoritative voice of the living God, Yahweh presents himself as someone who can impart life to bones. He alone can open figurative graves in which have been laid a future certainty (v. 13). He can and will do these things because he is the God of the authoritative "I will," which is an expression used six times in three verses (12–14): "I will open your graves"; "[I will] raise you from your graves"; "I will bring you into the land"; "I will put my Spirit within you"; "I will place you in your own land"; and "I will do it." His promise is indeed a hope settled and secure.

3) To renew in his people an inward experience of God's divine favor—in other words, to restore life to their dead and dried "bones,"

the Lord God promises to put his breath within them (v. 14). This breath, of course, is the same breath that imparted life to Adam in the original creation (Gen. 2:7). Here, at the dawn of a new work of God in which he will bring his exiles back to the land of Jerusalem, this breath is the inward seal of God's outward covenant love. To paraphrase the text (Ezek. 37:14), God will put his breath of life within them and raise up their souls, and they shall indeed know life.

All this is a sweet and rich foreshadowing of what God will do in the new covenant, of which Ezekiel has just spoken in the previous chapter (the heart of that covenant is found in 36:24–28). And to that second and fuller meaning of Ezekiel's vision, we must now turn.

The Dry Bones and the Christian Imagination

As I have argued, the first meaning of Ezekiel's dry bones vision is to provide real and lasting hope to the refugees in Babylon. But since there is dual authorship of Holy Scripture, there is always the possibility of a second and fuller meaning to a text, even in one like this, which was already prophetic at the time of its writing.

On its surface, the vision of dry bones comes across to us today like an amazing Christian trailer, a prerelease clip of the resurrection of the just at the end of the age. And in two different ways, there is an unavoidable connection between this prophetic vision and the post-Easter reality of the Christian faith. The first has to do with God's "resurrection capability." Ezekiel is asking his contemporaries to imagine a world in which God is able to do what is the "impossiblest" thing, to raise dead corpses to life. To be more stark, he is asking them to imagine a world in which God is able to raise corpses that have been dead so long that they are just piles of sun-bleached, dry bones with no flesh on them at all. The spiritual benefit of imagining such a God is immense. If and once the exiles have done so, and if and once they have believed in their hearts that the Lord God has this sort of beyond-the-bounds, life-rendering power, then it would be an easy step for them to find hope in the midst of their exile. Regardless of their actual situation and its existential impact, God will give new life. His new-covenant promise of giving them such life by putting his Spirit (breath) within them can be counted on. He is the Lord of such miracles. He can, if he chose, restore dead bones to physical life. How much easier to restore their hearts!

But to say that the Lord God *can* raise the dead to life is not the same as to say that he *will*, any more than to say that God can create a pink zebra is not the same as to say that he will. Divine capability and divine promise are two different things. But the wonder of this dry bones vision is that it brings both capability and promise together. It not only captures us with a vision of God as the one who can give life to the dead; it presents him as the one who will do so. In a way that Babylonian exiles could never have imagined, Ezekiel's vision promises the supreme event of the new covenant, the impossiblest thing in history, the resurrection of Messiah and his people from the grave.

This promise of resurrection is the second way in which Ezekiel's vision connects to us today. To show that it is indeed there in the text, take a look with me at what I call the "annex" to the main vision, verses 12 through 14. A shift takes place between verses 11 and 12, one subtle enough to be easily missed but not so subtle as to lack a textual marker. In verse 12, the Lord God commands Ezekiel yet again to speak, and to do so he uses the formula "prophesy, and say." The formula has been used twice before: in verse 4, as the Lord directs Ezekiel to speak to the bones; and in verse 9, as he directs him to speak to the breath/wind. Here in verse 12, he is directing Ezekiel to speak to "the whole house of Israel" (v. 11). As was the case in each of the previous two visionary moments, there is a shift in focus. Specifically, here the scene changes from standing in a valley of dry bones to standing in a quite different place. That may be surprising, given that the scene in verses 1 through 10 is admittedly the most memorable if not the weightiest part of the vision, with its piles of bones and resurrected army. But the sheer mass of that vision should not overshadow the change in verse 11; from this point on through verse 14, we are no longer in the valley. Instead, we are in a graveyard. Ezekiel wants us to know that; four times in verses 12 and 13 the Lord God uses the word "graves."

The repetition of the word "graves" highlights in neon yellow a dramatic refocus. Whereas in the initial valley vision (vv. 1–10) the resurrection involved the bony, unburied remains of some great Jewish army, now the resurrection involves the buried remains of all the people of Israel, present and future. So while one can read this closing annex of the prophecy in a figurative way, as speaking of the restoration of life to the "bones"—the heart and soul—of the exiles, the fourfold use of "graves" signals that a different scene is before us. This is especially the case in light of the resurrection of Jesus Christ from the dead. In verses 12 through 14, we have a straightforward if easily overlooked appeal to read the annex, if not all fourteen verses of the vision, as a call to believe in a future resurrection of the body. Especially when you feed the preceding valley vision into the annex, this resurrection is presented like nowhere else in Scripture: in detailed physicality, bone by bone, with God's Spirit superintending in all his regenerative power.

Ezekiel's vision of the dry bones and the graveyard is a treasure for our Christian imaginations as much as it was a treasure for the despairing exiles in Babylon. God presented to them the world of what *could* be through his impossiblest power. God presents to us the world of what *will* be through Christ's resurrection and the certain hope it gives us. And it is these two ways of connecting the text to our imagination, what could be and what will be, to which we now turn.

Colloquy

For a moment, review the results from your imagination audit, the exercise we proposed at the end of chapter 3. In particular, focus on what you learned about the life-sucking, God-displeasing images you jotted down. Consider their range, their force, and their impact on your heart. As you do so, you probably feel like the Jewish exiles in Babylon: "My imagination can be so God-forsaken. It may have its better moments, but overall it is an agent of the world, the flesh, and the Devil. So it's not surprising that my affections for Christ and his kingdom (my "bones") so often feel dried up and dead. Is there any hope for change?"

An honest confession to God (and to others as appropriate) is the place to begin if you are serious about renewal. God's Spirit, the great gift of his new-covenant promise, has been pledged to you, and he will, as Ezekiel says, "remove the heart of stone . . . and give you a heart of flesh" (Ezek. 36:26). And the first step toward that impossiblest transformation is to acknowledge our iniquity and ask God to sprinkle "clean water" upon our imagination, cleansing it from all its "uncleannesses" and all its "idols" (v. 25).

The apostle Paul has this sort of deep transformation in mind when he asks us to count ourselves "dead to sin and alive to God in Christ Jesus" (Rom. 6:11). And as a first intentional step of that Christ-centered faith, he instructs us to present ourselves "to God as those who have been brought from death to life," and to present to him our "members" (which includes our imagination) as "instruments for righteousness" (v. 13). Take note of that last word: "righteousness."

A redeemed imagination is a *righteous* imagination. As we already discussed in chapter 3, the prevailing tendency in our time is to give the imagination a free pass when it comes to matters of moral responsibility and righteousness. In part this is the case because we don't pay attention to our imagination (see chapter 1). It also may be a matter of false belief: functionally, we believe that our imagination is an unwieldy beast subject to all sorts of emotional confusion and subconscious impulses that cannot be controlled. "It's gonna do what it's gonna do, so why bother?"

So let us say it again: a redeemed imagination is a righteous imagination.

And righteous imaginations are the work of the Spirit of God. He sometimes works miraculously; that's why from time to time you will meet (and perhaps envy) a Christian who testifies that "God took away all my memories of past sin when I trusted Christ." But more often the Spirit of God works righteousness through our choices. As Paul puts it, again in Romans, believers are "by the Spirit" called and empowered to "put to death the deeds of the [sinful] body" (8:13).

So how does one do this in relation to the imagination? In our experience, we have found that a righteous imagination is the result of a righteous "imagination feed" kept strong over time. We mentioned the concept of imagination feed in the last chapter, where we described it as the network of visual or mental input, behaviors, relationships, and unopposed ruminating thoughts that feed your imagination. It's like the RSS feed to your homepage, with the obvious difference being that the real-time input is being streamed into your mind, where it is stored for later use by the imagination, whether good or bad.

One of the most strategic Spirit-led decisions you can make about your imagination is to establish and maintain a righteous feed over time. It's the old GIGO rule of computer programming written onto our souls: "garbage in, garbage out." What you put in is what you will get out. What you sow is what you will reap. So with that rule in mind, below are three sets of practical suggestions on establishing and maintaining a God-honoring feed.

1) Visual Input

We all face daily choices of what TV shows and movies to watch, where to surf on the web, and what pictures to settle our gaze on. By God's grace and gospel, turn away from the "old" and pursue the "new." Apply God's righteous standards here. And do so remembering that your choices, whether sinful or Christ-honoring, will not only affect you in the moment of decision; they will also feed your imagination for the future. The bad has a way of turning up, say, four days later unexpectedly; the good, thankfully, does too. So choose your images with the long view of building a righteous imagination.

2) Mental Input

For the believer, nothing has more power to settle and direct the imagination than God's Word. We have already encouraged you to meditate daily on God's Word. To that we add an equal appeal to memorize God's Word. The Gospels especially, with their vivid pictures of our Savior, have a way of strengthening a righteous imagination.

3) Opposing Ruminating Thoughts

We have all been subject to video or audio brain-files that play endlessly in our minds over the course of a morning or a day or a week or even longer. "Earworms" are what they are called when they are mostly audio, whether music or speech. But there are eyeworms as well, things like a scene from a movie or a replayed event from the past or a dreaded outcome in the future. Our imaginations are held captive. On the one hand, if the worm is Christ-honoring, then count it a blessing—as long as you can pay attention to the task before you without distraction. But if the worm is defiling, then the rumination must be battled. If my (Matt's) experience is any indication, you do best to fight fire with fire. In other words, you will have to displace the corrupt worm with a better and stronger worm. As the apostle Paul might say, if you really want to put something off, then you will have to put something on in its place.

This is where your imagination audit can be of value, especially the second step. Take what you learned about patterns and similarities and turn them to your advantage. Does music help you get rid of a worm? Does reading the Word? Does sharing your struggle with another believer? Does getting together with other believers in order to "pursue righteousness, faith, love, and peace" (2 Tim. 2:22)? Use as many weapons as you can in the fight for a righteous imagination.

In closing, we want to underline the importance of establishing and maintaining a righteous imagination feed *over time*. What we sow to our imagination we will surely reap. Earlier, I (Gene) mentioned William Wordsworth, one of the greatest poets in the English language. Perhaps his most famous short poem has to do with seeing some "golden daffodils" in bloom. He writes about their beauty in that particular moment, but he then adds something else:

> I gazed—and gazed—but little thought
> What wealth the [flowers] to me had brought.

He goes on to explain that at those times in the future when he might be "in vacant or in pensive mood," the daffodils could "flash upon [his] inward eye," rescuing him from the despair or confusion of the moment.

Wordsworth is articulating the power of a righteous imagination feed—in this case connected to beauty, the inseparable cousin of righteousness. What we are saying is, establish and strengthen over time a righteous imagination feed. While not the only way, this is the normal way for the Spirit of God to do the impossiblest thing, to give life to our imagination where formerly there was death.

Lord, we thank you for what we can do with our imagination. We can recall experiences that we have had in the past. We can project things that might happen in the future. We can contemplate the present. We can conceive of things that do not exist at all. Help us in our imaginings, that they be righteous and that they glorify you. So shape our imagination that it enables us to see all of life in the light of the revelation of your Word and the resurrection life we have in Jesus Christ. In whose name we pray. Amen.

5

Imagination and the
Community of Grace

Everything will live where the river goes.

Ezekiel 47:9

Gandalf! I thought you were dead! But then I
thought I was dead myself. Is everything sad going
to come untrue? What's happened to the world?

Samwise Gamgee, hobbit, in *The Return of the King*

From Gene

So imagination is an important God-given, human power. We can
sin and become idolatrous in our imagination, from which we construct false worldviews. But our imagination can also shape our ethi-
cal life in a good way, making us compassionate toward others and
enabling us to serve our neighbors in a forward-looking way. And a
Christian imagination is key to the formation of a Christian worldview. Imagination plays an important spiritual role in meditation,
contemplation, and prayer. And, as Matt will show as he explores
Ezekiel's final vision, God's Word reaches us in the very depths of our
heart by addressing our imagination.

But what do we mean by a "Christian imagination"? How do we acquire one? And what do we do with it?

The Christian Imagination

On one level, the imagination as a human faculty is the same for Christians and non-Christians. What Coleridge called "the secondary imagination"—the creative powers, memory, fantasizing, and other abilities to conceive mental images as we choose—is much the same for everyone, though some people, such as artists and inventors, have extraordinary gifts and talents in these areas. But "the primary imagination"—by which we make sense of what we perceive—has to do with worldview. This deeper imaginative faculty has some universal qualities that are innately human, and it also has qualities that are unique to each individual, such as the personal memories and experiences that help make up our identities. But our view of the world, the model through which we interpret our experiences and initiate our actions, is a function of our most profound and internalized beliefs. So we can speak of a "Christian imagination," which is a function of the Christian worldview.

James Sire, in his classic book on the subject, *The Universe Next Door*, analyzes the various worldviews, including that of "Christian theism," in these terms:

> Each worldview considers the following basic issues: the nature and character of God or ultimate reality, the nature of the universe, the nature of humanity, the question of what happens to a person after death, the basis of human knowing, the basis of ethics and the meaning of history.[1]

He goes on to describe the Christian perspective: ultimate reality is the infinite, personal God, who is both transcendent and incarnate; the universe is his creation; human beings were made in his image and yet are fallen, so are both valuable and sinful; after death is an eternal life in hell or in heaven; we know by our God-given reason and by his revelation in his Word; right and wrong are transcendent and grounded in God's character; history is linear, meaningful, and tied to God's purposes.[2]

So the Christian imagination, seeing God as the ultimate reality, would gratefully receive the natural world as God's creation, would see other human beings as worthy of both love and suspicion, would apply the moral truths of God's Word, and would sense that life has meaning. The person who imagines in these terms would use them to interpret and to see the meaning in everything that happens. And any expression of that person—whether an e-mail message or a work of art—any engagement of the creative, secondary imagination, would likely manifest that same Christian imagination.

Acquiring a Christian Imagination

A Christian imagination comes from internalizing Christian truth, not just from knowing a set of doctrines abstractly. They have to penetrate deeply into the heart and become part of one's identity. The way that happens, again, is through the imagination.

The Bible awakens the imagination of those who read it. It can, as we say, "capture the imagination." God's Word uses imaginative means—recounting true stories, accounts of people's lives, parables, descriptions, visions, symbols, and typology—so that its truths, through the Holy Spirit, cut deep, "piercing to the division of soul and of spirit" (Heb. 4:12). Thus, a Christian imagination comes, above all, from reading the Bible continually, studying it, meditating on it, and just saturating your mind and your imagination with the Word of God.

There is a difference between religions of the Word and religions of the image. Media scholar Neil Postman explores the implications of the prohibition of graven images in the Ten Commandments, contrasting the image-centered pagans with the God of the Jews, "who was to exist in the Word and through the Word."[3] As our culture today becomes increasingly visual—television, movies, the computer screen—the mind-set formed by graven images (emotionalism, immediate gratification, anti-intellectualism) is coming back.[4] Christians must remain people of the Word and thus of language. But language is precisely what stimulates and feeds the imagination. When we watch video images on a screen, we are receiving images that have already been manufactured for us, the production of someone else's imagination. When we read a story—whether in a book, online, or on Kindle—our own internal imagination is at work. There is, indeed, a place for visual images. But a distinctly Christian imagination is formed best by language—reading, listening, conversation.

The Bible says that we are to "hear" God's Word. That apprehension of language surely includes reading. We know that the ancients read aloud, even when they were reading to themselves, so that they would hear themselves reading.[5] Language in its essence is an oral medium to be received aurally. Actually listening to God's Word as it is spoken aloud can be especially powerful. Traditionally, this happened in church. The old liturgies and Protestant orders of worship included extensive and systematic Bible readings. Hearing God's Word also happened in the context of preaching God's Word. In a sermon, a text from the Bible is focused upon, explained, and applied, often appealing to and awakening the listeners' imagination. Thus, hearing good preaching week in and week out can profoundly shape a Christian worldview and a Christian imagination.

In fact, involvement in church—worshiping, participating in the sacraments, receiving teaching, studying the Bible, and experiencing fellowship with other Christians—is critically important. Worldviews have a strong social and cultural component.[6] We pick up our ways of thinking and our ways of imagining, in part at least, from the people around us and from the communities that we belong to. A social group with a common history and a common identity constitutes a culture. A person might have a number of cultural back-grounds (being at once, say, an American, a southerner, of Italian heritage, and of the Millennial generation). The role of culture can be exaggerated, as in the postmodernists' belief in cultural determin-ism (the notion that culture determines everything about us). Still, culture in the sense of belonging to extended communities is surely a gift of God, who made us social beings ("It is not good that the man should be alone" [Gen. 2:18]). Every culture has its customs, tradi-tions, rituals, and lore through which it is defined and transmitted from generation to generation.

Religion plays an important role in culture. Most world religions are inseparable from a particular culture, which they support by giving them a divine significance (Hinduism in India, Islam in Arab nations, animism in tribal societies). Christianity is unique in that it is not sim-ply a cultural religion but a universal faith that is for "every tribe and language and people and nation" (Rev. 5:9). There has always been the temptation to turn Christianity into just another cultural religion, one that exists to give a sacred status to America or England or the Holy Roman Empire or Western civilization. This is generally manifested in bad theology and cultural idolatry. But since Christianity applies to "every tribe and language and people and nation"—all of which are cultural categories—it has an impact on all of the cultures it touches.[7]

In a different way, the Christian church is also a social group with a common history and a common identity, and thus the church has a culture of its own. For all of the diversity in the church, all Chris-tians throughout history tend to have a common worldview and a common spiritual, intellectual, and artistic heritage. On a much smaller scale, individual churches, as social groups, constitute a sort of mini-culture of their own. This is true of denominations (urban ethnic Catholics, Southern Baptists, WASP-ish Episcopalians) and local congregations (friendly suburban megachurches, small rural churches, urban store-front communities, aging inner-city parishes), with each individual congregation having its own personality that comes from its particular collection of members.

But far beyond the social community of a church is the spiritual reality that binds individual Christians into a unity far more profound than any mere cultural identity:

> For just as the body is one and has many members, and all the members of the body, though many, are one body, so it is with Christ. For in one Spirit we were all baptized into one body— Jews or Greeks, slaves or free—and all were made to drink of one Spirit. . . . God has so composed the body, giving greater honor to the part that lacked it, that there may be no division in the body, but that the members may have the same care for one another. If one member suffers, all suffer together; if one member is honored, all rejoice together. Now you are the body of Christ and individually members of it. (1 Cor. 12:12–13, 24–27)

Notice how this text refers to something tangible that incorporates all Christians in all of their diversity into one body: baptism. Two chapters earlier, the apostle Paul talks about the Lord's Supper in similar terms, a "participation in the body of Christ" that incorporates us all into his body, the church: "The cup of blessing that we bless, is it not a participation in the blood of Christ? The bread that we break, is it not a participation in the body of Christ? Because there is one bread, we who are many are one body, for we all partake of the one bread" (1 Cor. 10:16–17). Certainly there are different theological understandings of the sacraments, whether baptism and the Lord's Supper literally incorporate us into the body of Christ (as we Lutherans believe), whether the references are only symbolic, or some other point on that spectrum. Either way, we see God, the creator, using "visible words" (as the Reformers called the sacraments) that impress upon us flesh-and-blood human beings the reality of the gospel in tangible terms that have great imaginative resonance.

Imagination and the Community of Grace

The point is, life in the church at every level will help you cultivate a Christian imagination. This includes worship, of course and
above all, but also participating with your fellow members in the
potluck dinners and Bible studies, service projects and fellowship
activities, that make up the ordinary life of the congregation. But
it also means drawing on the larger universal church that stretches
back over time and many cultures, reading the great theologians and
devotional writers of the past—from your theological tradition, to be
sure, but also others—listening to the great Christian composers and
enjoying the work of Christian artists and authors of all ages. This is
to draw on the Christian heritage, which will shape your worldview
and your imagination in profound ways.

I would add that contemporary Christians are acting recklessly
when they completely jettison the old hymns, the classic orders of
worship, the theological language, and the various traditions of their
churches. To do so cuts off Christians from the Christian culture.
I know the reasons: "But the unchurched don't know what all of
that means!" So they need to be taught that meaning and initiated
into that community that transcends time and space. The early
church turned gladiators, courtesans, and Stoic philosophers into
Christians by means of careful catechesis and incremental stages of
initiation. A congregation that makes contemporary culture normative over Christian culture—to the point of replacing it—will teach
its members to have contemporary worldviews and a contemporary
imagination.

Does this mean that Christians should take in only works of the
Christian imagination? That they should avoid writings, art, and artifacts that are expressions of other worldviews? Not at all.

Reading through a Worldview

Remember that a worldview is something that we see *with*, a model
by which we "view" the "world." So someone with a Christian world-

view is able to look at all the world and everything in the world—including the constructions of non-Christian worldviews—in the light of Christian truth.

Someone without a fully formed Christian imagination—a young child, for instance, or a new convert—would likely find it difficult to form one out of an imaginative diet that consisted of nothing but non-Christian or anti-Christian expressions. Consuming nihilistic arguments, reading nihilistic novels, and listening to nihilistic music is likely to orient a person's imagination to nihilism. And yet a person with a fully formed Christian imagination and worldview can look even at nihilism from a Christian perspective.

One of my literature students recently told me that he just could not handle the works of Ernest Hemingway. They were too dark, too existentialist, for him to take in without shaking his faith. That student showed a commendable sensitivity to his spiritual state. And yet I myself read Hemingway with great profit. That his characters are always trying to live by their own moral codes in a morally empty universe is sheer existentialism, but to me, as a Christian reader, Hemingway just proves that no one can escape the moral law, including those who do not believe in it.

When I read the ancient pagans such as Homer and Virgil, I feel no temptation to adopt their polytheism; rather, their imaginative universe—in which the gods are unrighteous and care little for human beings, in which all of the dead go to hell, and in which individuals struggle futilely against an indifferent fate—helps me appreciate how Christianity came as such good news to the ancient world.

When I read works from the Christian eras (remember, I am a literature professor by trade), I see the Christian influence everywhere. Certainly some of the greatest imaginative works—Dante's *Comedy*, Milton's *Paradise Lost*, the poetry of John Donne, George Herbert, and Gerard Manley Hopkins—are explicitly Christian and are rich explorations of Christian truth and the Christian life. Even non-Christians (such as Christopher Marlowe) are often operating within a Christian worldview, which enables them to create works from what is essentially a Christian imagination (such as *Dr. Faustus*). Being a Christian (having saving faith in Jesus Christ) and having a Christian worldview (a biblical perspective on all of life) are two separate things. Just as a new convert, while truly being a Christian, may lack at first a Christian worldview, someone educated in the Christian tradition, surrounded by Christians, and immersed in a Christian-influenced culture may well think and imagine in Christian terms, despite embracing sin and rejecting God. Thus, much of Western literature manifests a generally Christian worldview—depicting fallen human beings struggling in a meaningful and morally charged universe—even when its subject matter seems secular, in not explicitly raising religious issues. The works of William Shakespeare, Jane Austen, and Charles Dickens are all animated by an underlying Christian worldview. You wouldn't get your theology from them, something they hardly address, but they can build up your Christian imagination.

Someone told me, "I don't read anything published after the nineteenth century." That might work as a rough rule of thumb for the extent of a dominant Christian imaginative consensus, though it was already coming unraveled and had been since the eighteenth century. And even authors writing in modern and post-modern times often draw on the capital of their Christian heritage. I think of Faulkner, who plunges into the hearts of his characters, and Steinbeck, with his use of biblical imagery and story lines, and Borges, with his philosophically penetrating speculations. In fact, the best authors, the aesthetically most sophisticated, tend to be the most honest and thus often align more with Christian truth, as compared with writers who try to surf the shallows of the culture in order to make the best-seller lists.

But, again, the Christian imagination allows me a way of approaching and benefiting from works that emerge out of a non-Christian worldview. When I read non-Christian Romantics such as Shelley or Whitman, I appreciate the beauties and mysteries of nature that they evoke, filling me with praise for nature's Creator, while setting aside the authors' pantheism. When I read the nineteenth-century materialists, I see the human and social costs of Darwinism. When I read twentieth- or twenty-first-century nihilists, I am reminded what it is like to be lost.

I love virtually all satire—which, in ridiculing vice, assumes an objective moral standard[8]—and Dantesque comedy, which moves from pain to joy. I enjoy fantasy of all eras that awakens my sense of wonder.

This does not mean that I can read—or watch or listen to—anything and everything. I can handle the nihilists, when I have to read them as part of my work, but they seldom interest me. Some worldviews, such as New Agey mysticism and political utopianism, have nothing for me. Some works, such as comic routines, aspire to satire, but instead of ridiculing vice, as the genre demands, they ridicule virtue. I enjoy historical fiction, attempts to recreate something that actually happened with the use of fictional narrative techniques, but some efforts have a modern bias and distort history. Strangely, I find myself bored by nonstop action, especially in movies, what Milton called "tedious havoc."[9] So for these and many other reasons, lots of books—as well as movies and music—either put me out of patience or repel me. Christians will have different points of difficulty and levels of tolerance, just as they have different tastes.

All Christians should beware of fare that causes them to sin in their imagination—such as "obligatory sex scenes" that can verge on the pornographic. Taking too much pleasure in images of brutality can be a sinful indulgence. And false worldviews *that attract them*, that pull them away from Christian truth, should be avoided. The focus should be not just on the content of a work—whether it refers to sex or describes violence or has non-Christian ideas—but on the *effect*. Is it presenting elements that I can relate to objectively, or is it affecting me in a harmful way?

A good guide here is the familiar text from Philippians, which, however, I think is often misapplied:

> Whatever is true, whatever is honorable, whatever is just, whatever is pure, whatever is lovely, whatever is commendable, if there is any excellence, if there is anything worthy of praise, think about these things. (Phil. 4:8)

If something is "true," from whatever source, it is of God, since he created everything that exists. If something is good ("honorable," "just," "pure"), from whatever source, it is of God. If something is beautiful ("lovely," "commendable," "excellence," "worthy of praise"), it is of God. Here are the three classical absolutes—the true, the good, and the beautiful—and they all derive from God and point to him. Therefore, they are the domain of God's children. We are to "think about these things," and thinking involves not only the reason but also the imagination.

One word in this passage is often neglected, though it is repeated six times: "whatever." This is not the "whatever" of postmodern relativism that assumes one expression or set of beliefs is just as true, good, or beautiful as any other. Nor is it the "whatever" of boredom or apathy. This is the "whatever" that opens up everything to the Christian.

> For all things are yours, whether Paul or Apollos or Cephas or the world or life or death or the present or the future—all are yours, and you are Christ's, and Christ is God's. (1 Cor. 3:21–23)

"All things are yours"! Because "you are Christ's"!

I have nothing to fear from other worldviews, because mine is bigger than all the others, containing their truths and filling in their blind spots. The Christian imagination is vaster than those that derive from narrow human frames of reference. The Christian imagination comprehends both the depths of human wretchedness and the heights of human greatness, the whole range of emotions from agony to joy, despair to ecstasy, the created universe in all of its order and its mystery.

"All things are yours"! Because "you are Christ's"! Imagine that.

From Matt

Transformation

Of all the hundreds of stories about Augustine of Hippo, my favorite is one that took place shortly after his conversion. The news of Augustine's newfound faith had not yet been canvassed throughout Milan, so on one particular day, as the young Christian walked past a former sexual partner without acknowledgment, she turned toward him and called, "Augustine, it is I."

Augustine, who presumably had recognized her but did not know how to handle the awkwardness, turned back and, rephrasing her comment, answered, "Yes, I know. But it is no longer I."

Wow! What a story! Part of me—the undergraduate degree in English literature side—applauds the ease with which both the unnamed woman and Augustine handled the first-person pronoun. "It is I," they said. Neither slid into the casually ungrammatical "It is me." They both knew their Latin and English (smile) well; they had mastered the subjective case.

More seriously, however, what stands out in the story is the transforming power of the gospel. The man who would become one of history's most influential thinkers and theologians had been changed by Christ. His desires had been crucified with Christ so that it was no longer "I who live, but Christ who lives in me" (Gal. 2:20).

This same theme, the transforming power of the gospel, lies at the heart of the final vision of Ezekiel. It is the largest of all Ezekiel's visions, comprising eight chapters, from Ezekiel 40:1 all the way to 48:35, the very last verse in the book. Most of the vision takes place in and around a reconstructed Jerusalem temple as imagined by the prophet. Ezekiel and his angelic guide remain inside the city walls for most of the time, examining and measuring the various gates, chambers, and regulations of this future temple. Near the very end of the vision, however, the two travel outside the walls in order to follow the course of a river issuing from the city. It is a strong and rushing river that began as only a thin trickle spilling from the east side of the temple building. Their journey along the banks of the ever-widening river allows them opportunity not only to measure it and wade into it; they also discuss its transforming impact on animal life and human culture. As the angel says in 47:9, "Everything will live where the river goes."

It is this smaller vision within the vision (47:1–12), rather than the entire eight chapters of Ezekiel's temple vision, that will be my focus in this closing chapter. I have made that choice for several reasons, chief among them the unforgettable power of the gospel truths pictured by the prophet here. As I will show, this temple river and the blessing it brings are dynamic symbols of the new-covenant blessings that will be given to God's new-covenant people for the blessing of the world.

But I get ahead of myself. Before we dig into the temple river, let's take a look at the historical background of this final vision of Ezekiel.

A Swan Song—with a Twist

As is typical in his other prophecies, Ezekiel gives us a precise date for this fourth vision. According to 40:1, the "hand of the Lord" came upon the prophet. Much like the second vision, he was picked up from Babylon and carried hundreds of miles to the west to Jerusalem, the city that "was struck down." The date? April 28, 573 BC. For Ezekiel, that would be "the twenty-fifth year of our exile, at the beginning of the year, on the tenth day of the month" (v. 1).

Once you do the math, you realize that this date has important biographical significance. Ezekiel was now about fifty years old. He had spent the first half of his life in Jerusalem, training to be a priest in what is now a destroyed temple. The second half had been spent in Babylon, where some twenty years ago, around the time he should have begun his ministry as a priest had he not been exiled, he was called to be a prophet. For the two decades since, he has served the Lord God faithfully in this different vocation. And what a vocation it has been! The prophet has experienced three massive visions. He has staged a series of sign acts that mark a high point in Old Testament prophetic theater. He has pronounced oracles of warning, rebuked leaders, prophesied the collapse of Jerusalem, offered the hope of a new covenant, and judged pagan nations.

So it is into this sort of mix that his final vision comes.[10] In fact, apart from one small prophecy that would come two years later (29:17–21),[11] this would be Ezekiel's final gift to his fellow exiles. If tradition is to be relied upon, Ezekiel was martyred in Babylon by his own people some two to three years after his fourth vision, around the year 570 BC. Not surprisingly, therefore, his tomb is supposedly located in a small village of what is today southern Iraq.

Practically speaking, Ezekiel's fourth vision is his swan song—and a much needed one at that. Along the lines of his third vision, the prophet seeks to offer hope to the exiles, particularly in light of what has become a painfully apparent set of facts: God did not intervene when the Babylonians laid siege to Jerusalem, and as a result the holy city and its most holy temple were ruthlessly destroyed. All that took place some thirteen years ago, and since then the Lord God has not revisited his people to restore the city and its temple to their former splendor. The harsh realities of the exile and the divine chastisement behind it have truly set in.[12]

It is a critical time in the history of faith among God's people. So once again God goes after the hearts of his people in exile. The divine strategy to do this should be recognizable by now: the way to the heart is through the imagination. So God works through his prophet, not, as I have argued throughout this book, with an oracle or a parable or some other form of verbal communication but rather with a vision. And it is a protracted vision at that, one that fills up nine chapters in our Bibles (chapters 40 through 48 inclusive). That amounts to 260 verses, which is longer than Ephesians and Philippians combined! In fact, this vision is the longest in the Old Testament, and in the New Testament is exceeded in length only by the unbroken vision that we call the book of Revelation.

Now one might think that given its length, this vision would have had a telltale effect upon its hearers. I know that if I preached an extra-long sermon, I would do so with the hope that my congregation would take note and respond. And yet nothing happens as a result of Ezekiel's vision. It seems that it was to no effect. I say that because, in one of the odd twists about this fourth vision, none of the exiles attempted to build out its blueprint when they returned to Judah after King Cyrus's decree in 538 BC (Ezra 1:1–2:70). Quite to the contrary, when the foundation of the second temple had been completed, there was "the sound of the people's weeping" (Ezra 3:13), not because the outline in no way matched what Ezekiel had mapped out in his prophecy (Ezekiel 40) but because it was as nothing in comparison to "the first temple" (Ezra 3:12). In other words, it was the still-held memory of Solomon's temple that worked in the collective consciousness of the exiles, not the marvelous radiance of Ezekiel's vision. The same could be said for Isaiah's and Micah's shared vision of a temple mountain that would one day fill the earth (Isaiah 2; Micah 4); people classified it in a different category. They acted as if there was some shared understanding that these visions were about something other than the physical building in Jerusalem—or at least something other in this age.

The returned exiles' tears over the unimpressive second temple is a significant piece of a bigger story of which the exiles were unaware. Sure, the grand promises of a glorious restoration after the exile seemed to get off to a great start when God intervened.[13] The mighty Cyrus issued his decree, and the people began to return to the land! But in time it became evident that these prophetic promises were not being fulfilled as envisioned. For example, only a remnant returned to Judah, not the whole nation. Consequently, Judah remained a button-sized province and a vassal state at that. The foreign control continued for centuries, on through the time of Jesus the Messiah. Further, Ezekiel's temple was not built, the land was not reallocated along the lines of Ezekiel's prophecy, and an amazingly glorious Jerusalem was not restored under the rule of an equally glorious king.[14]

But this seeming shortfall of the promises surrounding the exiles' return was not a final failure after all. In fact, through it God introduced a reversal component in the grander story line of his redemption. By that, I mean that the pitifully small beginnings set the stage for the launch of the true fulfillment, that is, the arrival of the true Messiah and the inauguration of an entirely different kingdom under his reign. As G. K. Beale puts it, "The major irreversible features of the restoration promises begin fulfillment in Christ's coming."[15]

So what is the point of Ezekiel's fourth vision if it is not about a second temple to replace Solomon's once the exiles return? More particularly, what are we to make of the river that flows from its eastern side? And what value do the answers to these questions have for the Christian imagination?

Thankfully, scholars have written hundreds of pages on these issues—at least on the first two. So in the few pages ahead I will tap into their key ideas by making connections between Ezekiel and four other people. I will do so in order to show the rich significance of the river vision to the Christian imagination. Specifically, I will show that the primary force of the river vision for us today is symbolic. It displays imaginatively rich truths about the gospel, its impact upon the church, and through the church its impact upon communities. The place to begin all this, oddly enough, is with a seeming red herring: Ezekiel's relationship to Moses.

Ezekiel and Moses

I am convinced that in the overall flow of redemptive theology in the Bible, Ezekiel plays an important but underappreciated role, and this role comes to the foreground in his final temple vision (chaps. 40–48). To state it in a glaringly provocative way, in his temple vision Ezekiel functions as a new Moses for a new era in God's plan. In anticipation of the new covenant that will be signed, sealed, and delivered by the Messiah, God has Ezekiel rework the old covenant, especially its Mosaic legislation and Jerusalem-based worship system. If you think about it, you would almost expect such a reworking now that the temple and Jerusalem have been razed. The Lord God himself has appeared to Ezekiel in sovereign glory on the plains outside Babylon. Long gone is the temple-based vision of God's glory that came to Isaiah.

So Ezekiel reworks the Mosaic covenant. He does so at the macro level. We do not have in Ezekiel 40–48 a replacement for the Ten Commandments or a detailed Book of the Covenant or a Levitical code in all its painstaking details. But in the big sweep, at the macro level, we do have a new set of regulations for a new era in Israel's history. In particular, Ezekiel's temple vision provides:

- a revised blueprint for the temple (chaps. 40–42), replacing the tabernacle plan that Moses received in Exodus;

- a modified set of festivals (45:18–46:18), which includes a heavy emphasis on the role of a messianic figure that Ezekiel refers to as "the prince";[16]

- a resetting of the priestly line (44:15–31); and

- a new division of the land (47:13–48:29).

And, in a move to seal the legitimacy of Ezekiel's new order, the *shekinah* glory of God, which had filled the first temple and then departed in judgment (chap. 10), returns in all its splendor as part of Ezekiel's vision (chap. 43).

For Ezekiel's fellow exiles, these new-Moses components of his final vision must have been yet one more outrageous event in his already over-the-top career. Did he really consider himself to be on par with Moses? Was there no end to his reach?

Perhaps Ezekiel's purpose behind the seeming overreach was a pastoral one. Perhaps he intended to stop the exiles in their tracks and force them to think about their own lives and the law of Moses. Perhaps the prophet hoped for some sort of broad-based self-examination and repentance.[17] But there is no indication that such repentance ever took place.

Why this vision of a new temple, then, if it did not have some short-term reconstruction project in mind? In more modern times, the solution to the quandary for some has been to locate the vision's fulfillment in a future millennial age. I, for one, was taught precisely that approach back in the seventies and eighties. As a result, when I came to chapters 40 through 48 of Ezekiel, my eyes would gloss over and my mind would shift into neutral. I had no answer to the questions, "Why nine chapters filled with extravagant if not obsessive details about something that is totally in the future? Wouldn't one or two chapters be enough?" These were years when I was a young Christian, so there was a certain amount of self-centeredness in my complaint. But still, I was groping with a legitimate question of proportion. Nowhere else in Scripture could one find such an extended vision about something that had no direct bearing on either its first hearers or Christ's followers today.

Now, I am not one to dismiss a future and millennial fulfillment of this vision, especially when a wide range of scholars argue for it.[18] But the fact still remains that Moses was on his way out. The Mosaic era with its system of laws and worship was becoming a thing of the past. That was the case historically: the temple had been destroyed, sacrifices were no longer being offered, and the glory of God itself had appeared to God's prophet in, of all places, Babylon. But that was also the case prophetically. Ezekiel himself, along with his senior contemporary Jeremiah, had spoken of a new covenant that would replace the old, a covenant that would not settle for external obedience. Instead, it would move down to the heart and work from the inside out. "I will put my Spirit within you, and cause you to walk in my statutes and be careful to obey my rules" (Ezek. 36:27).

It should be no surprise, therefore, to find all sorts of precursors to this new covenant embedded in Ezekiel's temple vision. In its elaborate appeal to the imagination, the prophet signals that the old is passing, that changes are coming, that God's covenant structure will shift, and that preparations have begun for the new era of the new covenant. In our own age, with the help and guidance of the Spirit, one's imagination can find beautiful anticipations of the "grace and truth" that John's Gospel speaks about—grace and truth through Jesus Christ that upended the law "given through Moses" (John 1:17).

This is certainly the case with Ezekiel's vision of a flowing river. It has taken on a life of its own with respect to the Christian imagination, and for good reason. Once we understand it for what it is, the river vision powerfully captures us with vivid pictures of the gospel's impact. As the angel says, "Everything will live where the river goes." The angel's words describe the river of God's gospel grace that flows from the side of the new temple, Jesus's body, through his people and into the world. I do not hesitate to make such bold connections between what is for many an obscure and gnarly Old Testament text and the clean-cut blessings of the gospel. Other prophets have already done the same.

Ezekiel and Zechariah

Take Zechariah, for instance. He was one of the Babylonian exiles who returned to Jerusalem sometime around 538 BC in response to the decree of Cyrus. He was young at the time. It was his grandfather, Iddo, who led the family back; Iddo is mentioned by name among "the priests and Levites who came up with Zerubbabel" to the land of Judea (Neh. 12:1–4). According to Zechariah 1:1, the prophet began his ministry some eighteen years later, in 520 BC. That would mean that Zechariah's ministry came some fifty years after Ezekiel's river vision of 570 BC. Although it is a matter of conjecture, it seems reasonable to connect these dots and understand that Zechariah heard about Ezekiel's vision from his grandfather, who would have been alive at the close of Ezekiel's ministry.

As far as the texts of Zechariah and Ezekiel go, the dots connect well. So, for instance, the book of Zechariah makes abundant use of Ezekiel's apocalyptic style. Like his predecessor, Zechariah used it in the opening chapters of his book to point the returned exiles to the future. In part, he sought to console their dejected hearts with visions of future glory. But he also warned them about the deep grief of God over their meager faith. From Zechariah (again, like Ezekiel) the returned remnant heard about God's uncompromising holiness and his impending judgment. They were asked by the Lord to repent, to "return" to him that he might "return" to them. They had described to them in vivid terms a period of final tribulation that would then issue in the day of the Lord.

With that as a background, the closing chapter of Zechariah puts forward a grand vision of the day in which Messiah will come and reign as king. Among the predictions made is one that repeats and expands upon Ezekiel's temple vision. "On that day," Zechariah 14:8 reads, "living waters shall flow out from Jerusalem, half of them to the eastern sea and half of them to the western sea. It shall continue in summer as in winter." The prophet speaks of a healing stream, one that, just like Ezekiel's river, flows with healing powers to the east, all the way out to the Dead Sea, as well as to the west, to the Mediterranean.

"Living waters" is Zechariah's shorthand for Ezekiel's original image. Most likely there is a play on the word "living." The phrase describes what we would call "flowing waters," waters that do not sit and stagnate and choke out life but instead bring moisture and growth and cleansing and physical health for all. But "living waters" also describes a river that brings life in other senses too: physical life, yes, but also spiritual life. And it is this sense of "living waters" that lies behind the words of yet another prophet.

Ezekiel and Jesus of Nazareth

"Living waters" is exactly the phrase that Jesus uses to describe the new-covenant gift of the Spirit. In the seventh chapter of the Gospel of John, Jesus says, "Whoever believes in me, as the Scripture has said, 'Out of his heart will flow rivers of living water'" (v. 38). The way Jesus refers to "the Scripture" rather than to a particular text or book seems deliberate, since there is no one verse that lies behind his quotation. Instead, Jesus is compiling a set of three Scriptures: the Zechariah allusion just mentioned, Joel 3:18,[19] and of course the much longer vision in Ezekiel 47:1–12.

"Living waters" is an apt phrase for the new-covenant gift of the Spirit, for the Spirit is indeed poured into the hearts of those who trust him (see Acts 2:17) in order to flow out from them into the lives of the people around (see Acts 2:38). Ezekiel's vision of the small trickle that issues from under the temple and then travels outward, transforming everything in its course, could not be a more appropriate picture of such gospel influence. Like Ezekiel's stream, the Spirit is first poured out as a "trickle" upon a small group of 120 gathered disciples on Pentecost. But through that 120 the trickle becomes a rivulet when over three thousand hear Peter's first gospel sermon and, cut to the heart by the Spirit's convicting work (Acts 2:37), trust Christ and are added to the church. The rivulet becomes a stream as thousands more come to Christ in the course of the book of Acts. The stream grows broader and deeper when another stream joins it, the stream of gospel outreach to the Gentiles through Barnabas, Paul, and others. And then missionary journey by journey, imprisonment by imprisonment, within decades the combined streams become a river pouring across the Roman Empire. Within a hundred years of Christ's resurrection, the gospel has spilled out and over the Mediterranean world, across to Asia, and then funnels down through centuries of history to every continent (including Antarctica!) around the globe.

And so the link between Jesus's promise in the Gospel of John about the rivers of water and Ezekiel's river vision (along with the briefer texts of Zechariah and Joel) is sharpened to a point when you take Ezekiel's words into the realm of Christian imagination. The river vision has found a major piece of fulfillment in the outpouring of God's Spirit upon his people. There is more fulfillment to come once the Messiah returns and establishes his kingdom. But like so much else in the New Testament work of the Messiah, the age of fulfillment has already been inaugurated and in an unexpectedly different sort of way. Ezekiel's temple and river have become, for now, the new temple of the people of God, from whom the river of the Spirit and his grace flow to the parched world around them.

This is certainly what the apostle Paul had in mind when he expanded upon Jesus's link between Ezekiel's temple and the Holy Spirit. What was present as seed in Jesus's words grows into stalk, branch, and flower in Paul's writings. Perhaps the most obvious and profound application of temple imagery to the church is in the book of Ephesians: "In whom [that is, the Messiah Jesus] the whole structure [that is, the church] . . . grows into a holy temple in the Lord" (2:21). Paul has caught the imagination side of Ezekiel's temple well. New Testament theologian Gregory Beale expands upon this statement of Paul's and in doing so echoes Ezekiel's vision in Babylon:

> God's revelatory presence in the form of the Spirit will no longer be located in the holy of holies of Israel's temple but instead will break out of its architectural shackles in the eschaton and spread throughout the earth. The true temple and true place of worship . . . can be found wherever the extending form of God's . . . presence in the Spirit goes and among whoever is included in its sphere.[20]

Certainly Ezekiel's river vision presents to the Christian imagination a motivating picture of what Beale describes. "There is a river whose streams make glad the city of God" (Ps. 46:4), the gospel of grace with its transforming power. Let me briefly show you four ways by which this vision inspires our imagination with Christ and his gospel.

Where the River Begins

Ezekiel's river, which eventually becomes a raging torrent, begins as a trickle from "below the threshold of the temple" on the south end of the eastern side (Ezek. 47:1). Note right away that the water comes forth from underneath the temple itself. Ezekiel recognizes a deep source for the water: beneath the temple. In light of the Old Testament understanding that the temple is God's throne on earth, the water comes from below the very seat of earth's heavenly king. It comes from below the house where God dwells, the place where his people gather to worship and where sacrifices are offered by the priests. It is truly the "river of God," for is there anything that could belong to God more than a river that issues below his feet?

And it issues on the southern side of the temple, the side in the past that had never been a likely source of water. So there it is, God's river, originating from beneath his feet in an unexpected manner. For the Christian imagination, how rich a picture of Calvary! The river of God's grace originates from beneath the feet of the Messiah, who himself was put to death in the most unlikely of means, crucifixion, and in the most unlikely of places, a hill outside Jerusalem.

How the Water Expands

Ezekiel's river gets deeper and wider as it flows eastward from the temple. At first it is just a trickle. At fifteen hundred feet from the temple, it is ankle deep. Go another fifteen hundred out, and it is knee deep. Another fifteen hundred, and it is waist deep. Another fifteen hundred, and Ezekiel cannot pass through it.

The deepening of the river answers to another movement. The river expands as it moves away from a place that Ezekiel has portrayed as increasingly narrow and restrictive. Back in chapters 40 through 42, the staircases from temple court to temple court go up and up as you go further into the complex. Furthermore, the doorways get smaller and smaller. Not just anyone can get to the heart of this temple: only one person, Jesus Christ. From him, the unique priest, pours forth an expanding river.

And so it has been through history since Christ's ascension. From the trickle of believers that followed him in Acts 1, the Christian movement has indeed become a torrent that has continued to deepen and expand. As a result, it is not at all unusual for someone to attend a Christian conference, as I recently did, and find himself seated at a table of six, which, in addition to this white Causasian from Princeton, New Jersey, included Narni from Jakarta, Mary from Hong

Kong, Steve from South Africa, Felix from Malawi, and Kate from Ghana by way of London.

How the River Reverses Nature

In the unforgettable opening sequence of *The Empire Strikes Back,* robotic probes are dispatched from an imperial star destroyer across the entire galaxy. They drop into every location that might serve as a hideout for Luke Skywalker and the rebel alliance. The scene is vividly filmed, with the probes curving out and downward from the mother ship, silently and irreversibly speeding to their programmed destinations.

In a similar way, Adam's disobedience has fanned out across all creation. From a single choice in a single moment at a single place, sin has fanned out and dropped down into every place, every event, and every human heart. "Oh wretched people that we are! Who will deliver us from this body of death?" (Rom. 7:24 AT).

But the river of God's grace, flowing out from his holy presence, pouring through the combined lives of his people, the church, brings healing, hope, food, and life to the fallen and cursed world. Salt water becomes fresh (Ezek. 47:8), every dry and dying pond becomes alive, fish will multiply, and the catch will be great (v. 10). Again, there is an abundance of food for thought—better, food for the imagination—in this grand picture of Ezekiel's. Among others, John dipped deeply into this river when he wrote the closing scenes of Revelation. Chapter 22 borrows heavily from Ezekiel 47, transposing the image of the healing river into the opening scene in Genesis of the garden of Eden. The future age of the church and the world will fulfill these luxuriant scenes and their promises of a transformed world.

In the meantime, however, believers are called to live their callings in this age in light of the age to come. Their lives are to be based upon an already enthroned Christ and his already launched kingdom, by whom the blessings of his future age are to be tasted, lived, and poured out into the world around. Believers today are called, like Ezekiel, to be "sons of Adam."

How the River Belongs to the "Son of Adam"

Ezekiel's favorite name for himself is "son of man." I guess, to be more precise, it is God's favorite name for Ezekiel, since virtually all of the ninety-three times the name is used in the book, it is on God's lips. It is his preferred way of addressing the prophet. In point of fact, the name is used only two other times in the Old Testament, a fact that reinforces the importance of the name to Ezekiel's identity.

"Son of man" is the standard English translation of the Hebrew phrase *ben-adam*. If you're like me, your eyes just jumped over those italicized words. "Why bother with the linguistic specifics of all this?" But go back and read that Hebrew phrase again: *ben-adam. Ben*: "son of." *Adam*: man, or, just as valid, Adam—as in the name of the first man. "Son of man" is in fact always a reference to our first father. "Son of Adam," then, is God's preferred name for Ezekiel. Of all the Old Testament heroes and prophets, godly kings and serving priests, there is only one who is repeatedly identified that way. It's Ezekiel, the "Son of Adam."

The point should not be ignored. Throughout the entire book, and at least once in this vision of the flowing river, there are allusions to events surrounding the first Adam. For example, like Adam Ezekiel has God breathe his Spirit into him (Ezek. 2:2). And like Adam, Ezekiel is presented with garden trees from which he can eat (47:12).

What I am getting at is this: Ezekiel, the son of Adam, functions as a transitional figure in the flow of the covenants. As a recipient of four remarkable visions, two having to do with the future, he is an early member of God's new community, one marked by a new temple and a restored land and a great prince, the Messiah. Of course it wouldn't be until the New Testament that an explanation of how a man like Ezekiel, sinful and dwelling among the sinful exiles, could become a member of that new community, own the new name "son of Adam," and be a member of a newly created people. But like so much else in the book, and definitely in the temple vision with its running river, Ezekiel is anticipating the blessings of the age to come through his intensely symbolic and apocalyptic visions.

And chief among those blessings is the forgiveness of Messiah's new covenant. The river vision tells us of a forgiveness that expands as it flows from Jerusalem—a forceful contrast to the ever-shrinking doorways of approach in the envisioned temple. And through this forgiveness there is transformation. Salt becomes sweet, the lost becomes found, and the enemies become friends, as the New Testament community of faith takes the gospel from Jerusalem to Judea, Samaria, and the ends of the earth.

The imaginative implications of Ezekiel's river vision are rich and stirring, for, as we shall now see, forgiveness received leads to forgiveness extended, and through that process the bitterness of the world is sweetened. With this in mind, let us now turn to the community dimensions of the Christian imagination.

Colloquy

Brian Uzzi lives in Chicagoland. He is the Richard L. Thomas Professor of Leadership and Organizational Change at Northwestern University's Kellogg School of Management. Back in 2005 he published the results of some out-of-the-box research on the social dimensions of human imagination, in particular its creative side. Uzzi studied the connections between friendship, collaboration, and creativity involved in the 2,258 musicals that were staged on Broadway between 1877 and 1990. One of his findings was a concept he has labeled "Q." "Q" has nothing to do with the proposed origins of the New Testament Gospels; instead, it is Uzzi's measure of the degree of friendship and social interconnectedness among the people involved in any given musical. Low-level "Q" correlated to those musicals that failed; they didn't have the zing and zest of musicals produced by a team with a higher "Q," a team where people felt comfortable with one another, safe in sharing ideas, excited to work together, and free to speak their mind. On the other hand, though, if "Q" became too high—if, in other words, the team members became too familiar and too predictable, the musical was also likely to bomb. Apparently the absence of fresh ideas from people who were new to the team and would therefore drive "Q" down a bit was a different but equally real liability.[21]

So what's the point of connection between Uzzi and Ezekiel, between Uzzi and the Christian imagination? Simply this, that imagination does not do well in isolation. Christians' growing in the ability to use imagination to the glory of God is a community project. The redeemed imagination flourishes in a situation where we are in relationship with both people we know and trust and people who are new and becoming known. To put it simply, imagination should thrive in the fellowship of the local church. A healthy local church provides a rich combination of relationships, some old and some new, some as easy as a close family and others involving people who are different, perhaps radically different. The sociology of the Corinthian church is a case in point: slave and free, Jew and Gentile, wealthy and poor, male and female, followers of Paul and followers of Peter—the list goes on and on. It was a church with a rich diversity of "Q," a collage of old and new relationships growing together in the grace of God.

Alas, for many the local church is an impediment to the imagination. As I (Gene) will demonstrate in the next chapter, far too many young adults are leaving the church today because of its "lack of compassion" (that is, imagination applied to human relationships), its "hostility to the arts" (imagination applied to the world around), and its "lack of vision" for the world outside its doors (imagination applied to the lost). Upon such young adults the vision of Ezekiel's river is lost. The thought of a river of grace spilling out from the church to them and their contemporaries, sweetening the bitter and bringing life wherever it flows, such a thought is, well, imaginary.

For these and all sorts of other reasons, it is our conviction that churches need to do a more intentional job of cultivating the redeemed imagination among its members. The failure to do so is already taking its toll, as above, while the benefits of doing so are exactly what the gospel is about. Shaping a gospel vision in church members, forming the imagination around the difference the gospel can make—these activities are essential to Christian discipleship. As James K. A. Smith, professor at Calvin College, argues in his *Desiring the Kingdom*, we human beings are first of all lovers. We are "creatures of desire who crave particular visions [read, imagination's pictures] of the kingdom." Smith contends that the activities of gathered Christian worship ("liturgies") shape "the visions of the good life," and those visions in turn "shape and constitute our most basic attunement to the world."[22]

Not surprisingly, we agree. The role of the imagination is critical. Through deeply seated pictures it brings together mental process and emotional force, shaping us to be lovers of God and neighbor first of all, as opposed to simply receptacles of theology (as good and necessary as it is) or doers of deeds (as good and necessary as they are).

The church stands to benefit in every way by being intentional about the cultivation of a redeemed imagination among its members. Here are three practical ways to do it:

1) Make it a point to learn together how to listen to Scripture well. Listening with attention and focus is a lost art today. This is especially true in our sermon-downloadable age, where the focus can easily shift to the preacher's words as opposed to God's Holy Word. I (Matt) am a preacher; I have preached God's Word to a growing congregation in Princeton, New Jersey, for nearly thirty years. So believe me when I say, I believe in preaching. But I also believe in the power of God's Word, and I tremble to think that people are unintentionally losing a reverential respect for Scripture itself. We need to relearn how to listen to Scripture with fresh ears and allow it to speak directly to us. As Psalm 119; Colossians 4:16; and Revelation 1:3 make plain, hearing the words of God is an essential mark of the Christian and the church.

Listening to Scripture with fresh ears is in good measure a work of imagination. That is obviously the case when the texts being read are from books filled with historical accounts: the Gospels, Acts, or the Old Testament history books. But with practice it can also be the case with Paul's letters, the Psalms, the Wisdom Literature, and the Prophets. Especially when one's eyes are closed, the mind begins to connect the words to pictures. Over time we learn how to weave the judging part of our minds into the hearing and imagining process so that together they can strain out the bad and redirect us toward the good.

So we encourage the rise of groups that meet weekly to listen to Scripture together. A simple pattern for such a group is to begin with prayer and then listen for ten minutes to an Old Testament passage. Allow there to be up to ten minutes of narration after the listening. By "narration" we mean explaining to the group what you heard and saw as the text was read. The reading of a New Testament text follows, this time a bit longer, between fifteen and twenty minutes. Narration follows, and the session comes to a close with a brief prayer.

2) Encourage church leadership to draw a connecting line between the church and the arts. Beauty and art were God's inventions in the first place. Sadly, the church has not always made this connection. But it's a connection that needs to be made at all times, and especially in these days. As a measure of the importance of the arts in today's society, consider these statistics from Tim Keller's *Center Church:* "According to the United States census, between 1970 and 1990 the number of people describing themselves as 'artist' more

than doubled, from 737,000 to 1.7 million. Since 1990, the number
. . . continued to grow another 16 percent to nearly two million."[23]
For both theological and cultural reasons, therefore, it is important
for churches that love Christ and his gospel to draw an unbroken
line connecting them to the arts. There are different ways of doing
this, but perhaps the simplest is to start a support group for artists
(broadly defined so as to include not just visual artists but musicians,
writers, actors, singers, architects, graphic designers, etc.) and those
interested in the arts. If the first few meetings could include a short,
interactive message from a church leader on an art-related biblical
theme ("Genesis 1 and God's creativity"; "the beauty of holiness"),
the line connecting the church and the arts will be drawn with extra
boldness.

   3) Preach with the imagination in view. Remember that the mental pictures we carry inside our minds, the vision we have of God or
of the church or of the good life—these pictures are where life makes
up its mind. Jesus understood that, and he therefore filled what we
call his "Sermon on the Mount" with vivid pictures ("a city on a hill"),
humorous images ("the log in your own eye"), instructive metaphors
("knock, and it will be opened"), and brief stories ("a foolish man
who built his house on the sand"). He appealed to the imagination
to engage, shape, and direct the mind.

   Likewise for us preachers (Matt speaking): make sure that your
preaching is not limited to propositional content alone. Propositions
must be connected to life and heart, and one of the best ways to do
that is through the imagination. So don't use just illustrations. Work
on metaphors. Compare the point you are making to something you
see or taste or hear. Appeal to the senses in your descriptions. Include all the senses as you imagine the biblical scene behind the
text you are preaching. Block the scene out in the space around the
pulpit. Map it for the congregation. And make sure that you don't
just preach the Epistles, as necessary as they are. Remember to sup-

plement them with texts from the more explicitly visual portions of Scripture. By that we mean the Gospels with their stories, the history books with their unforgettable characters, Genesis with its arche-typal plots, and the prophets with their vivid visions. Here's a challenge: why not preach Ezekiel? We're not saying the whole book, but how about a sermon series on Ezekiel 1—God? Or Ezekiel 8—sin? Or Ezekiel 37—hope? Or Ezekiel 47—communities of grace? Why not? God captured his prophet through the imagination way back then; he can still do it today.

O, Lord, we praise you for engrafting us into the church, your body. Thank you for our brothers and sisters in our local congregations, in our nation, and around the world. Thank you for our brothers and sisters throughout the ages who are already with you. Thank you for the way you feed and nourish us by means of pastors and preachers, the members of our Bible studies, and other fellow Christians, including those who are no longer on earth but whose words and wisdom live on in books that we can read and imagine. Help us and help our churches to cultivate our imagination so that a Christian worldview animates every part of our thinking and perceiving and so that the gospel of Jesus Christ penetrates the deepest recesses of our being. In his name we pray. Amen.

Conclusion

Imagination and Apologetics

Late have I loved you, O Beauty so ancient and so new; late have
I loved you! You were within me, and I was outside; and I sought
you outside and in my loneliness fell upon those things that you
have made. . . . But you called to me and cried to me and broke
my deafness; you sent forth your beams and shone upon me and
chased away my blindness; you breathed your fragrance upon
me, and I drew in my breath and now I pant for you. I tasted you,
and now I hunger and thirst for you.

Augustine, describing his heart before and after his conversion

From Matt

When I was seven years old, I climbed a pine tree one rainy day after
school. At its top, I peered into a bird's nest in which I saw three
eggs, each a blue reflection of a clear New England sky. As a result,
I became a Christian.

Sort of. There were some eleven years between the nest and my
conversion, and there were many bigger and more consequential issues at play when I came to faith in Christ, not least of which was
the gospel itself, which has nothing to do with bird eggs. But in the
transition from a dead faith to a living one, the role of my imagination cannot be ignored.

Let me explain. The nest I discovered that afternoon was a robins' nest. And therefore the three eggs were a delicate sky blue, well set off by the wet, black bough and dark needles of the pine tree. So vivid was the scene that my imagination still remembers it. And for good reason, because when I reported my find to my mother, she apparently thought it important enough to warrant a trip to the bookstore downtown where she purchased the little *Golden Guide to Birds.* And when she brought it home, wouldn't you know, the background color of the guide was the same as the eggs in the nest. And, as if all were part of some grand conspiracy, the two birds on the cover were robins!

I was hooked: the climb, the joy of discovery, the wonder of three eggs so perfectly shaped and exquisitely colored, the special moments of learning shared with my mom, and the robins. All that was the beginning of my lifelong fascination with birds. To this day, I am so taken by them that I am absolutely clueless as to why anyone would not love them as much as I do. After all, birds fly (and who wouldn't want to fly?), birds are beautiful to behold (and who doesn't love to see something beautiful?), and birds sing (and who doesn't like music?).

But to the main point: it was my love of birds that landed me in the text that the Spirit would use to bring me to faith in Christ. It happened this way. At age eighteen, in the final few weeks leading up to my conversion, I was in dialogue with many different Christian friends. One in particular knew of my love for birds and commented that Jesus had some interesting things to say about them.

"Where? And what did he say?" I asked.

She turned me to the end of the sixth chapter of the Gospel of Matthew. There, in the middle of the Sermon on the Mount, Jesus encourages his followers to trust God concerning all the details of their lives. And one way he drives home his appeal is by turning attention to birds: "Look at the birds of the air: they neither sow nor reap nor gather into barns, and yet your heavenly Father feeds them" (Matt. 6:26).

Needless to say, I was captivated by the text. Jesus spoke to my bird-filled imagination. I bracketed the entire paragraph in the Bible I had begun reading at the time. And my friend then commented, "You know, there's another text in the Gospel of Matthew that I think you will like just as much."

"Oh, what's that?"

"It's at the end of the eleventh chapter."

And so I was led to the passage that God's Spirit would use a few weeks later to draw me to faith in Jesus Christ, Matthew 11:28–30. It, too, appeals to the imagination, this time by using a metaphor drawn from the work world to describe the soul without Christ's rest: "Come to me, all who labor and are heavy laden, and I will give you rest" (v. 28). As with Matthew 6, I was taken. Christ was speaking to me, heavy as I was with sin and guilt. Several days later, and only by the grace of God, my life would be Christ's.

Imagination was the way into my heart. Like so many other people I have since met, my previous unbelief wasn't simply a matter of reasoned rejection of Christ—although that was a factor. There was more to it. To borrow the words of N. T. Wright in his little book on Psalms, I just couldn't imagine "what it might be like to live in God's world, in his time, in his space, and in his matter."[1] Jesus's invitation in Matthew 11:28–30 opened the door for me to imagine those very things.

From Gene

So the part of the mind known as the imagination—the ability to form mental images—is important in the life of the Christian. Though a realm in need of discipline and sanctification, the imagination is a God-given superpower, making possible some of the greatest achievements of human beings. It makes possible empathy and compassion, shapes our worldview, and is the way into our heart.

The imagination can also be the way into the heart of unbelievers. Many people in today's culture, trapped in their narrow materialistic worldview, "cannot imagine" any kind of spiritual reality. They perceive only dimly the difference between good and evil, and while they can respond to extreme cases of the two (they are human, after all), they have difficulty imagining themselves as sinners. God, Christ, hell, heaven, and redemption are outside of their imaginative frames of reference.

But it isn't just that they have trouble imagining spiritual reality; they have trouble imagining physical reality. Their world consists of material objects, which they are glad to use for their pleasure; but the objective universe has no meaning for them. They think science has not only explained the natural order but has explained it away. There is no mystery or wonder in the external world, only dead matter. It can be manipulated in various ways, but any kind of meaning must come from within the self. While there might be objective facts, there is no objective truth. They cannot imagine a creation, much less a creator.

One symptom of this tragic blindness is that people today are strangely impervious to reason. Rational arguments were important in the modernist era, which claimed the Enlightenment mantle of being the Age of Reason. But postmodernists often seem little affected by logic, chains of reasoning, or objective evidence.

Convincing people of the truth of Christianity thus poses new challenges today. Evangelists must try to reach people who have little conception of what the evangelists are talking about. Apologists can make superb arguments for the truth of Christianity that nevertheless fail to penetrate the mind-set of their audiences. To be sure, many are still coming to faith, proving that the Holy Spirit and not our merely human efforts is the one who brings people to Christ. And yet Christians must continue to speak about the objective truth of what we believe, objectivity being an important part of our worldview, both to emphasize to nonbelievers that the message of Christ is not just another construction of the self and to teach new believers how to think in objective terms. But one way to connect with postmodernists, to open their minds to a much larger worldview, is to reach their imagination.

What C. S. Lewis Did

C. S. Lewis is surely the best-known and most successful Christian apologist of the twentieth century. He showed that there is a rational case for Christianity. As such, he was addressing the modernist mind. And yet that was not all he was doing.

Consider the climax of his argument about Christ in *Mere Christianity*:

> A man who was merely a man and said the sort of things Jesus said would not be a great moral teacher. He would either be a lunatic—on a level with the man who says he is a poached egg—or else he would be the Devil of Hell. You must make your choice. Either this man was, and is, the Son of God, or else a madman or something worse. You can shut Him up for a fool, you can spit at Him and kill Him as a demon; or you can fall at His feet and call Him Lord and God.[2]

Here is a logical argument, establishing three possibilities and asserting which one is more plausible. But it is also addressing the imagination. When we read this argument, we are also picturing a lunatic, a Devil, and even a poached egg. We also picture in our minds the responses to Jesus: shut him up, spit at him, kill him, fall at his feet, call him Lord and God.

Lewis wrote many books that make the rational case for Christianity: *Mere Christianity*; *Miracles*; *The Problem of Pain*; *The Aboli-

tion of Man; *God in the Dock*; *Letters to Malcolm Chiefly on Prayer*.
His apologetic works are not abstract tomes, full of intellectual content but tedious to read. They are absorbing and hard to put down.
His reasoning, full of vivid illustrations and analogies, is compelling,
even exciting. This is because Lewis is stimulating not only his readers' intellect but also their imagination.

Lewis was also the author of fantasy novels: *The Chronicles of
Narnia*; *Out of the Silent Planet*; *Perelandra*; *That Hideous Strength*;
The Great Divorce; *The Screwtape Letters*; *Till We Have Faces*. At
a time when literary modernism favored works of grim realism,
Lewis was writing in the genre of untrammeled imagination. But
these works of the creative imagination, written to send their readers' imagination soaring, also were works of Christian apologetics,
playing a role, just like his rational arguments, in bringing countless
readers to faith.

An important clue to Lewis's life work can be found in the subtitle
of the first book he wrote after he became a Christian: *The Pilgrim's
Regress: An Allegorical Apology for Christianity, Reason, and Romanticism*. His is an apologetic not only for Christianity but also
for reason and Romanticism. But aren't reason and Romanticism
opposed to each other? How can he defend both logic *and* emotion,
realism *and* fantasy? And in what sense are both opposites under
attack and in need of defending?

This may be one of Lewis's greatest insights. The modernists, in
the name of reason, rejected Romanticism. Today's postmodernists,
in their subjectivity, reject reason. But even as early as 1933 when
Lewis published *Pilgrim's Regress*, both worldviews were taking
shape and starting to contend with each other. The narrow road
that the pilgrim must follow runs between two extremes. On one
side are barren, icy cliffs, symbolizing the cold, hard facts of rationalism. On the other side are hot, muddy swamps, symbolizing the
sensuality and inwardness of Romanticism. But when the pilgrim

finds Christianity, a true reason and a true Romanticism are restored to him.

Today, both objectivity and subjectivity are impoverished. Both are lifeless. Having no room for each other, they leave human beings trapped in a partial, incomplete state, with the different facets of their minds and personalities in conflict with each other. In the words of Lewis's rival and fellow convert T. S. Eliot, who put forward a similar diagnosis, human beings today are plagued with a "dissociation of sensibility," in which thinking and feeling—also reason and imagination—go in different directions.[3] Eliot found the unified sensibility he craved in seventeenth-century Christian poets such as John Donne and George Herbert, and then he himself embraced the Christian faith and experienced the wholeness it brings.

Lewis's own coming to Christ had its start in his imagination. What he presents in an allegorical fantasy in *The Pilgrim's Regress* and more straightforwardly in his autobiographical memoir *Surprised by Joy* is his account of various experiences of ineffable longing. These were moments of transcendence, glimpses of something beyond this life, which he felt as a mingling of joy and an almost painful yearning. As he recounts in *Surprised by Joy*, different things would bring on these feelings, but they were almost always works of the imagination: Beatrix Potter's *Squirrel Nutkin*; a recording of Wagner's *Ride of the Valkyries*; the mere title of William Morris's *The Well at the World's End*. A milestone in his spiritual pilgrimage was his discovery of *Phantases* by the Scottish clergyman George MacDonald, one of the great masters of Christian fantasy. When he read it, Lewis said, "My imagination was, in a certain sense, baptized."[4] Later, in a conversation about myth with his friend J. R. R. Tolkien, he realized that what he loved in myth—its aching beauties, its slain gods, its deaths and resurrections—pointed to Christ, in whom myth became fact.[5]

Imagination led C. S. Lewis to Christ, and he led others to Christ by awakening their imagination.[6]

Freeing Prisoners

Lewis's good friend and the man who brought him to Christ was J. R. R. Tolkien, an even greater writer of fantasies. In replying to the charge that fantasy is mere escapism, Tolkien asked, "Why should a man be scorned, if, finding himself in prison, he tries to get out and go home?"[7]

This is exactly the plight of the lost. They are prisoners of the sin that enslaves, to be sure (John 8:34). They are also imprisoned in their narrow, confining, claustrophobic worldview. That prison may be the materialism that insists that the physical world is all there is. Or it may be the even smaller and darker enclosure that is the self.

Tolkien wants to help the captive "get out" of his prison so that he can "go home." Imagining something bigger and better than the constricting confines of the prison blows out its walls. Imagination can also awaken a yearning for one's true home.[8]

To be sure, imagination can send an escaped prisoner in all kinds of directions, including to new imagination-created prisons. Christians must continue to insist on reason, evidence, and objective truth. What must be done is to reassociate truth and the imagination.

"Part of our problem in presenting the faith," observes Alison Milbank, "is that our world deadens desire, and many people do not know that they are missing anything."[9]

"For me," she says, "the whole enterprise of presenting the faith convincingly is aimed at opening this desire in others."[10] Helping people realize that they are missing something and awakening the desire for eternal life, for God, are critical for both apologetics and evangelism.

This is a task for the imagination but not at the expense of reason. But reason itself needs to be imaginatively rehabilitated. Again, Dr. Milbank suggests how:

Reason does need rescuing and we can do so by recasting the limit to understanding from a negation to an opening out to mystery. As Fr Giussani argues, reason discovers mystery: "the summit of reason's conquest may reveal itself as a foothill" but this perception is *itself* a positive discovery that there is more: "the existence of something incommensurable in relation to [Reason] itself." And it is imagination that helps reason to recognize the mystery *as* mystery. So let us use every imaginative tool at our disposal to awaken the religious sense, and then use reason to explain the difference this viewpoint makes to our experience of the whole of reality, which is restored to us, in all its fullness. [11]

A good example of how this apologetics of the imagination has worked in practice can be seen in this account from British journalist Miranda Threlfall-Holmes, who describes how, as an atheist, she was converted to Christianity through the poetry of George Herbert. (I have never understood why Herbert is so little known by evangelicals today. The Word of God is part of the texture of his verse, his major theme is the gospel, and few have written so profoundly of their "personal relationship with Jesus Christ." Also, even secular scholars agree on his stature as one of the greatest lyric poets of the English language in his formal and aesthetic mastery.)[12]

Ms. Threlfall-Holmes recalls first coming upon Herbert as a teenager in school. "By the end of the weekend, I realised that this poetry was the most dangerous challenge to my atheism that I had yet come across."[13] She says that she had assumed religion was for the weak-minded. "But here was some of the most fiercely intelligent poetry I had ever read, grappling with Christian doctrines and with a relationship with God. If this brilliant mind believed all this, and devoted a life to it, then clearly I needed to look at it again."[14] Notice that she is responding not simply to Herbert's imagination but also to his intelligence. And yet, her own intelligence needed something more.

She responds to the honest struggles that Herbert records. She says of his poems that "many of them clearly describe his intensely personal struggles with faith and calling. Even those that are more formal explorations of particular religious doctrines or concepts have a similar air of spiritual authenticity. There are no mere statements of dogma. The poems record the poet's own doubts and faith in a way that still rings true with many readers, even those with no explicit faith of their own."[15] She begins to see that there is more to Christianity than she realized.

> For Herbert, religion is never simply a set of dogmatic assertions, or a collection of cultural practices, as historical religion is sometimes caricatured. . . . It was easy to dismiss the truth of the 20 impossible things that religion seemed to expect me to believe before breakfast. It was much harder to dismiss my own emotional reaction to these poems: the beauty, the yearning, the enticing danger. They left me with the sense that I was standing on a cliff, staring out to sea, hearing marvellous tales of lands beyond the horizon and wondering if they were, after all, just fairy tales or whether the intensity with which the tales were told was evidence that the teller had indeed seen a barely imagined kingdom.[16]

Our churches are full of young people like teenage Miranda—smart, sophisticated in their own way, and eager to leave their parents' households—and we agonize how to reach and keep them. They need teaching, but simply throwing abstract doctrinal ideas at them may not be enough. The teaching needs to appeal to their intelligence. But Christianity is not merely about ideas. It is about mighty realities, as concrete as rough-hewn wood stained by blood. And Christianity is not about bourgeois complacency, but it addresses failures, suffering, and personal struggles. Teaching the faith to young people—or, for that matter, to the unchurched or to anyone today—should involve awakening them to "the beauty, the yearning, the enticing danger."

The point is not just that we need more poets and other artists like George Herbert, though we do. We do need more apologists like C. S. Lewis who can reach both the intellect and the imagination of people today, who are, in many ways, different from those Lewis addressed in his day. And we do need more writers like J. R. R. Tolkien who, even though they do not directly address religious issues, can expand the imagination of their readers and fill them with desire for realities beyond the world.

But we also need preachers who, much like Ezekiel, can move their hearers to a deeper response. We need people who can witness to their friends so that the message of the gospel is not easily dismissed but sinks in deeply. To be sure, the Word of God creates faith through the work of the Holy Spirit, but God's Word itself is much more than abstract ideas. It certainly teaches inerrant propositional truths, and it does so by means of historical narratives, parables, poetry, and figurative language—all of which address the imagination in the course of reaching the heart. Meanwhile, all Christians—especially as they face the dehumanizing, reductionistic, and materialistic mentality of our current times—need to love God with all their minds, which would include their imagination.

O, Lord, your Word describes those who do not know you as lost, as slaves, as dead. We were in that state, but you found us, freed us, and brought us back to life. Use us to bring the good news of your Son to those around us. Help us to find the right words to communicate your Word in its fullness and beauty. Awaken in those we seek to evangelize a yearning for everlasting life. Help them realize the ugliness of sin, the splendor of your created objective order, and the mystery of your incarnation, atonement, and resurrection. Raise up Christian writers, artists, thinkers, pastors, parents, and ordinary lay men and women who can communicate these wonders, as you have in the past. Meanwhile, give us a Christian, sanctified imagination that we may revel in all your works. Through Jesus Christ our Lord, Amen.

Notes

Chapter 1: Imagination: The Mind's Eye

1. *ESV Study Bible*, ed. Wayne Grudem (Wheaton, IL: Crossway, 2008).
2. Indeed, some have argued, not the least of whom was Augustine, that all of life is lived as a memory, an instantaneous and internal mental video capture of the external event that just took place. To the extent that they are correct, imagination is not simply pervasive; it is foundational and necessary to all of life experience.

Chapter 2: The Imagination and God

1. See my *Reading Between the Lines: A Christian Guide to Literature* (Wheaton, IL: Crossway, 1990), 20–23. Also my *Postmodern Times: A Christian Guide to Contemporary Thought and Culture* (Wheaton, IL: Crossway, 1994), 81–82. Both discussions draw on the work of Neil Postman. See also Arthur W. Hunt III, *The Vanishing Word: The Veneration of Visual Imagery in the Postmodern World* (Wheaton, IL: Crossway, 2003).
2. St. Augustine, *On the Trinity*, bk. 15, chap. 20, par. 39, in *Nicene and Post-Nicene Fathers*, First Series, vol. 3, trans. Arthur West Haddan, ed. Philip Schaff (Buffalo, NY: Christian Literature, 1887). Rev. and ed. Kevin Knight, http://www.newadvent.org/fathers/1301.htm>. Augustine's complete treatment of this subject is found in bk. 10.
3. *Summa Theologica*, pt. 1, q. 78, art. 4, in *The Summa Theologica of St. Thomas Aquinas*, trans. Fathers of the English Dominican Province (1920), online ed. Kevin Knight (2008) http://www.newadvent.org/summa/. Aquinas was in part drawing from Aristotle's *On the Soul*, bk. 3, pt. 3.
4. Martin Luther, "Against the Heavenly Prophets," in *Luther's Works* (Philadelphia: Fortress, 1958), 40:99–100.
5. Ibid., 100.
6. Louis L. Martz, *The Poetry of Meditation* (New Haven, CT: Yale University Press, 1954).
7. John Donne, "Holy Sonnet XIII," ln. 2, in *The Complete Poetry and Selected*

Prose of John Donne, ed. Charles M. Coffin (New York: Modern Library, 2001), 263.

8. Ibid., lines 5–8, 264.
9. Ibid., line 1, 263.
10. Ibid., line 14, 264.
11. N. T. Wright, *Acts for Everyone: Part 1* (Louisville, KY: Westminster, 2008), 138–41.
12. A. W. Tozer, *The Pursuit of God* (Harrisburg, PA: Christian Publications, 1948), 43.
13. See, e.g., the following: "Given the nature of the prophetic claim, the collapse of confidence in prophecy at [Ezekiel's] time involved necessarily a crisis of faith in the God in whose name the prophet spoke." From Joseph Blenkinsopp, *Ezekiel* (Louisville, KY: Westminster, 1990), 26. Blenkinsopp's volume is part of the Interpretation: A Bible Commentary for Teaching and Preaching series.
14. The term is not original to me. I have transposed it to my context from the writings of T. S. Eliot, major twentieth-century poet and literary critic, as we will discuss in the final chapter.
15. This unity of heart, mind, and body in service of the Father is a main theme of the Gospel of John. See, e.g., John 4:34; 6:52–59; 17:4–5.
16. The "Benevolent God" category and statistic are from Paul Fraese and Christopher Bader, *America's Four Gods* (New York: Oxford University Press, 2010).
17. Again, I borrow this phrase from the realm of literature. John Keats, one of the great Romantic poets of the early nineteenth century, spoke of the poet's "negative capability" in a letter to his two brothers in December 1817.
18. Quoted in George Marsden, *Jonathan Edwards: A Life* (New Haven, CT: Yale University Press, 2003), 495.
19. I am indebted to Christopher J. H. Wright for his analysis of the structure in this vision, along with his insightful details. See his excellent commentary, *The Message of Ezekiel: A New Heart and a New Spirit*, The Bible Speaks Today, ed. J. A. Motyer (Downers Grove, IL: InterVarsity, 2001).
20. Ibid., 49.
21. From Mather's *The Biblia Americana*, the earliest complete Bible commentary written in British North America (1693–1728). It is a six-volume commentary with a combined 4,500 pages on the entire Protestant Bible. These quotations are from a currently unpublished manuscript.
22. The verb used in Ps. 1:2 for "meditate" refers to a repetitive sound, whether of a dove's cooing, a lion's growling, or a human's muttering, talking to self, or speaking under one's breath.
23. See Louis L. Martz, *The Poetry of Meditation* (New Haven, CT: Yale University Press, 1976).

24. See, e.g., Kent Hughes, *Disciplines of a Godly Man* (Wheaton, IL: Crossway, 2001); or Doug McIntosh, *God Up Close: How to Meditate on His Word* (Chicago: Moody, 1998).
25. Tony Reinke, *Lit! A Christian Guide to Reading Books* (Wheaton, IL: Crossway, 2011), 83.
26. The four quotations are from ibid., 87 and 89.

Chapter 3: Imagination and Evil

1. "500 Greatest Songs of All Time," *Rolling Stone*, December 9, 2004, http://www.rollingstone.com/music/lists/the-500-greatest-songs-of-all -time-20110407/john-lennon-imagine-20110516. According to the magazine, the best song of all time is Bob Dylan's "Like a Rolling Stone." The second best is the Rolling Stones' "I Can't Get No Satisfaction."
2. See Charles Williams's imaginative exploration of this principle in his novel *Descent into Hell* (Grand Rapids, MI: Eerdmans, 1966).
3. A point Jesus himself continually makes, from the parable of the unforgiving servant (Matt. 18:21–35) to the Lord's Prayer (Matt. 6:12).
4. One other time Ezekiel is supernaturally transported from Babylon to Jerusalem, in chap. 40, at the start of his fourth vision.
5. The reference to Judah in Ezek. 8:1 seems at first glance rather dislocated, given that Ezekiel is in Babylon. Some have therefore argued that Ezekiel's vision took place before his deportation to Babylon, while he was still in Judah. But the subsequent description in v. 3, in which Ezekiel is seized by a lock of his hair, lifted up, and transported "in visions of God" to Jerusalem, with the city being explicitly named, indicates otherwise. The phrase "elders of Judah" is instead a reminder of the important and ongoing connection between the Jews in exile and the Jews in Jerusalem.
6. "Tammuz" is a reference to a Mesopotamian fertility deity who supposedly was slain by demons. The cultic rituals held in his honor included weeping for the god.
7. In an unusual moment of linguistic similarity across the ages, Ezekiel's terminology for "backs" has the equivalent nuance of the English "rear end."
8. That there is a demonic component to idolatry is evident in such texts as 1 Cor. 10:19–21.
9. The phrase is the title of Timothy Keller's book, *The Empty Promises of Money, Sex, and Power, and the Only Thing That Matters* (New York: Dutton, 2009).
10. And, as my bookshelves prove, I am among the last to want to deter anyone from buying and reading Brooks (*Precious Remedies against Satan's Devices*) or Owen or Baxter or Sibbes or any of the other Puritans!
11. Several centuries after Christ, the Desert Fathers would take the concept

of this Greek word, *logismoi*, and use it as a comprehensive term to refer to all the seductive products of our fallen imagination. Their reflections on this term would eventually lead to the medieval concept of "the seven deadly sins," and the more modern concept of root or habitual evil.

12. Excerpted from the TED Talk by Elizabeth Gilbert entitled "Your Elusive Creative Genius." The talk is worth listening to in relation to the material in this book. http://www.ted.com.

13. John Kleinig, *Grace upon Grace: Spirituality for Today* (St. Louis, MO: Concordia, 2008), 84–85.

Chapter 4: Imagination and the Future

1. See Samuel T. Coleridge, *Notes on English Divines* (Ann Arbor, MI: University of Michigan Library, 2009).

2. Samuel T. Coleridge, *Biographia Literaria* (Eugene, OR: Wipf & Stock, 2005), 114.

3. Thomas Kuhn, *The Structure of Scientific Revolutions* (Chicago: University of Chicago Press, 1962).

4. Christians should realize that any new scientific model might also pose challenges, albeit different challenges, to the biblical worldview. They also should avoid hitching their theological wagon to a particular scientific model, as the Roman Catholic Church did with the Ptolomaic cosmology. (Interestingly, a major center for the emerging Copernican cosmology was Luther's University of Wittenberg.) All scientific models, in my opinion, should be seen as heuristic and contingent, while still being useful and bearing elements of truth.

5. For a good overview of Kant's view of the imagination, see Douglas Burnham, "Immanuel Kant: Aesthetics," in *Internet Encyclopedia of Philosophy*, http://www.iep.utm.edu/kantaest/. For a more detailed treatment see Michael L. Thompson, ed., *Imagination in Kant's Critical Philosophy* (New York: Walter De Gruyter, 2013).

6. William Wordsworth, "Lines Composed a Few Miles above Tintern Abbey," lines 105–7.

7. Alison Milbank, "Apologetics and the Imagination: Making Strange," in *Imaginative Apologetics*, ed. Andrew Davison (London: SMC, 2011), 35. See also John Milbank's foreword to that volume, *xxii–xxiii*.

8. David K. Naugle, *Worldview: The History of a Concept* (Grand Rapids, MI: Eerdmans, 2002), 4. This important book shows how the concept grew out of Kant but has become a staple of many other schools of thought, including that of Christians from many different traditions.

9. James Sire, *The Universe Next Door: A Basic Worldview Catalog*, 5th ed. (Downers Grove, IL: InterVarsity, 2009).

10. Canadian philosopher Charles Taylor places heavy emphasis on the role of the imagination in the formation of worldview, particularly in relation to the rise of secularism. His massive work, *A Secular Age*, is brilliantly explained and summarized in James K. A. Smith's *How (Not) to Be Secular: Reading Charles Taylor* (Grand Rapids, MI: Eerdmans, 2014). See esp. chap. 2, "The Religious Path to Exclusive Humanism."

11. That is, the bones reassembled themselves as if they had a physician's knowledge of the human body, with each one correctly choosing and joining its correct "neighbor."

12. The cognate verb for "breathe" also occurs in v. 9, making a grand total of five uses of the word family in the single verse!

Chapter 5: Imagination and the Community of Grace

1. James Sire, *The Universe Next Door: A Basic Worldview Catalog* (Downers Grove, IL: InterVarsity, 2009), 27.

2. See ibid., 25–46.

3. Neil Postman, *Amusing Ourselves to Death* (New York: Penguin, 1985), 9.

4. See Arthur W. Hunt, *The Vanishing Word: The Veneration of Visual Imagery in the Postmodern World* (Wheaton, IL: Crossway, 2003).

5. See St. Augustine's *Confessions*, bk. 6, in which he marvels when he comes upon St. Ambrose reading silently. See also Alberto Manguel, *A History of Reading* (New York; Viking, 1996), 41–54.

6. See, e.g., Mary Clark, *In Search of Human Nature* (New York: Routledge, 2002), 2–11.

7. See, e.g., Alvin J. Schmidt, *Under the Influence: How Christianity Transformed Civilization* (Grand Rapids, MI: Zondervan, 2001).

8. See Dustin H. Griffin, *Satire: A Critical Reintroduction* (Louisville: University Press of Kentucky, 1994), 34–39.

9. *Paradise Lost*, bk. 8, line 30.

10. The vision, Ezekiel's last, came when he was fifty years old, the age at which a priest in Jerusalem would normally have concluded his years of service (Num. 8:25). Thus, the timing of Ezekiel's first and last visions, at ages thirty and fifty, corresponds neatly to the timing of his priestly service had he remained in Jerusalem.

11. Two years later, almost exactly to the day, i.e., April 26, 571. Oddly, the placement of this short prophecy does not follow the chronological order of all the other prophecies in the book. Presumably it should come at the very end of the book, after Ezekiel's temple vision. Instead, it is inserted in a set of prophecies that preceded the siege and fall of Jerusalem. These prophecies, and the one in question, all relate to judgments upon surrounding nations.

12. As a statement of the divine purpose of chastisement behind the exile, see, e.g., 2 Chron. 36:15–21.

13. See, e.g., the swelling prophecies of Isaiah 35 and 60.

14. See G. K. Beale, *A New Testament Biblical Theology: The Unfolding of the Old Testament in the New* (Grand Rapids, MI: Baker Academic, 2011), 172–73, for a fuller discussion of the absence of what he calls "irreversible features of the restoration promises."

15. Ibid., 173.

16. Ezekiel is loathe to use the noun *king* indiscriminately. From his standpoint, most of the last kings before the exile were not honorable or legitimate kings of the Jews. So, apart from a few odd references to King Jehoiachin (in the date formula of the opening verse of the book, in a reference to his being taken into exile in 17:12) and a nameless allusion to "the king" in a prophecy of judgment (7:27), no contemporary Judean ruler is called "king" except Jehoiachin. Ezekiel may have considered Jehoiachin in exile the still rightful ruler of Judah, hence his occasional use of the term in reference to him but his avoidance of it in relation to the final puppet kings of Judah. As an example, in 12:12 a prophecy is given that clearly refers to Zedekiah. It is precise enough to spell out that Zedekiah would attempt to flee Jerusalem once the walls gave way to the Babylonians. It also predicts that Zedekiah will somehow lose his sight as a result of the siege, which in fact happened (2 Kings 25:1–7). But in line with what has been said, Ezekiel refers to Zedekiah as "the prince."

17. This would not be the first time Ezekiel had such pastoral purposes behind outrageous moments in his ministry. See the call for repentance in Ezek. 6:8–10 that follows a bizarre prophecy against the mountains (not the inhabitants) of Israel!

18. Daniel Block, in his magisterial commentary *The Book of Ezekiel: Chapters 25–48* (Grand Rapids, MI: Eerdmans, 1998), discusses "ten factors one must consider in solving the riddle of Ezekiel's final vision" (p. 494). He also identifies key authors and works that represent the variety of interpretations (pp. 494–506).

19. "And in that day . . . a fountain shall come forth from the house of the LORD and water the Valley of Shittim."

20. Beale, *A New Testament Biblical Theology*, 135.

21. See Brian Uzzi and Jarrett Spiro, "Collaboration and Creativity: The Small World Problem," *American Journal of Sociology* 111 (2005): 447–504. We learned about Uzzi's work from a formerly published book by Jonah Lehrer, *Imagine: How Creativity Works* (New York: Houghton Mifflin Harcourt, 2012), 140–43. We say "formerly published" because the book has been withdrawn from sale and circulation. Lehrer apparently practiced a

little too much of what he preached; he creatively "imagined" some conversations involving musician Bob Dylan that never took place. Take heed: the dangers of the fallen imagination are equal-opportunity employers.

22. James K. A. Smith, *Desiring the Kingdom: Worship, Worldview, and Cultural Formation* (Grand Rapids, MI: Baker, 2009), 71, 25.
23. Timothy Keller, *Center Church: Doing Balanced, Gospel-Centered Ministry in Your City* (Grand Rapids, MI: Zondervan, 2012), 178.

Conclusion

1. N. T. Wright, *The Case for the Psalms: Why They Are Essential* (New York: HarperOne, 2013), 36.
2. C. S. Lewis, *Mere Christianity* (New York: Macmillan, 1968), 56.
3. See T. S. Eliot, "The Metaphysical Poets," in *Selected Essays 1917–1932* (New York: Harcourt Brace, 1932), 246–47.
4. C. S. Lewis, *Surprised by Joy* (New York: Harcourt, 1955), 181.
5. Ibid., 236.
6. See also Michael Ward, "How Lewis Lit the Way to Better Apologetics: Why the Path to Reasonable Faith Begins with Story and Imagination," *Christianity Today*, November 2013, 36ff.
7. J. R. R. Tolkien, "On Fairy Stories," *The Monsters and the Critics and Other Essays*, ed. Christopher Tolkien (Boston: Houghton Mifflin, 1984), 148.
8. This was what Lewis came to realize was the meaning of his experiences of "joy," as he explores in *Surprised by Joy* and dramatizes in *The Pilgrim's Regress*.
9. Alison Milbank, "Apologetics and the Imagination: Making Strange," in *Imaginative Apologetics*, ed. Andrew Davison (London: SCM, 2011), 35.
10. Ibid., 43.
11. Ibid., 44–45. Her reference is to Luigi Giussani, *The Religious Sense*, trans. John E. Zucchi (Montreal: McGill-Queens University Press, 1997), 117.
12. My first book, based on my dissertation, was about Herbert, and it has recently been rereleased. I commend it to you as a guide to this master of the Christian imagination: *Reformation Spirituality: The Religion of George Herbert* (Eugene, OR: Wipf & Stock, 2013).
13. Miranda Threlfall-Holmes, "George Herbert: The Man Who Converted Me from Atheism," *The Guardian*, February 17, 2014, http://www.theguardian.com/commentisfree/belief/2014/feb/17/george-herbert-dangerous-challenge-atheism.
14. Ibid.
15. Ibid.
16. Ibid.

General Index

Abolition of Man, The (Lewis), 145–46
Acts, book of, 130
Adam, 67–68, 134. *See also* fall, the
advertising, 94; and the Super Bowl, 94
Against the Heavenly Prophets (Luther), 38–39
Ai Weiwei, 21
animism, 113
Antony and Cleopatra (Shakespeare), 59
Aquinas, Thomas, 38, 88, 153n3
arts, the, and the church, 138–39
atheism, 60
Augustine of Hippo, 37–38, 120, 141, 153n2 (chapter 1), 153n2 (chapter 2), 157n5
Austen, Jane, 117

Babylon, 53; as the harlot of the book of Revelation, 53
Bader, Christopher, 154n16
baptism, 114
Baxter, Richard, 155n10
Beale, G. K., 124, 158n14
Beatles, the, 95
Beethoven, Ludwig von, 21
ben-adam (Hebrew: son of man), 134
Biblia Americana, The (Mather), 154n21

biblical meditation, 18, 54, 107; models for, 39–40, 55–56
Biographia Literaria (Coleridge), 86–87
Blenkinsopp, Joseph, 154n13
"bones," as an Old Testament figure of speech, 100–101
Borges, Jorge Luis, 117
Brooks, Thomas, 76
Bunyan, John, 17
Burnham, Douglas, 156n5
Bush, George W., 25
Buzi, 96

Calvin, John, 20, 48, 76
Center Church: Doing Balanced, Gospel-Centered Ministry in Your City (Keller), 138–39
Chariot of the Gods, The (von Daniken), 48
Christian imagination, 18, 110–11; acquiring a Christian imagination, 111–15; God as the starting point for, 45; how to cultivate a redeemed imagination, 137–40; as a resurrected imagination, 80; as a righteous imagination, 105–6. *See also* worldviews, the Christian worldview
Christianity, 113–14; spread of, 130, 132; as a universal faith, 113. *See also* theism, Christian theism;

General Index

Wilde, Oscar, 77
will, the, 14, 18; as fallen, 15, 61
Williams, Charles, 155n2
Word of God. *See* Scripture
Wordsworth, William, 86, 90, 108
worldviews, 60, 91–93; as caught
    rather than taught, 60; the
    Christian worldview, 91, 110–11;
    false worldviews, 60, 93, 118;
    the German *Weltanschauung*,
    91; how worldviews are shaped,
    92; as "interpretive paradigms,"
    92; materialistic worldview,

144; social and cultural compo-
    nent of, 112–13
Wright, Christopher J. H., 51,
    154n19
Wright, N. T., 44, 143

"Your Elusive Creative Genius" (Gil-
    bert), 156n12

Zechariah, 128
Zechariah, book of, 128–29; "living
    waters" in, 129
Zedekiah, 158n16

Scripture Index

Scripture Index

Scripture Index